the economics of
competitive coexistence

COMMUNIST ECONOMIC STRATEGY:

Soviet Growth and Capabilities

by

Alec Nove

NATIONAL PLANNING ASSOCIATION

Reports on

THE ECONOMICS OF COMPETITIVE COEXISTENCE

Communist Economic Strategy: The Role of East-Central Europe, by
Jan Wszelaki, xii and 132 pp., $3.00

Japan, China, and the West, by H. Michael Sapir, xii and 80 pp., $2.00

East and West in India's Development, by Wilfred Malenbaum, xi and
67 pp., $1.75

Communist Economic Strategy: The Rise of Mainland China, by A. Doak
Barnett, xii and 108 pp., $2.50

Communist Economic Strategy: Soviet Growth and Capabilities, by Alec
Nove, xii and 84 pp., $2.25

(Further publications in process.)

ii

CONTENTS

CONTENTS - 2

iv

BACKGROUND

Ever since the Soviet bloc began its trade-and-aid drive in the un-committed countries of Asia and the Middle East under the slogan of "competitive coexistence," Western statesmen and economists have been pondering its implications. How great is the capability of the Soviet bloc for a further expansion of these activities that cause so much concern in the West? What use is being made of the economic instrument in Soviet and in Western policy? What is the impact in the less developed areas and the effect on world trade and production?

The study of "The Economics of Competitive Coexistence" was proposed by the NPA International Committee and set up in 1956 as a separate project to investigate these questions and a host of related problems. As an aid to its forthcoming general volume of analysis the project has had prepared a number of country and area studies of which the present one on Soviet growth and capabilities is the fifth to reach the public. It is the third in the series on Communist Economic Strategy; with its companion pieces on East-Central Europe and Mainland China it is designed to throw some light on the Sino-Soviet bloc's capabilities of maintaining or expanding its current trade-and-aid offensive without thereby jeopardizing such other objectives as scientific and military advance, as well as accelerated economic growth.

The Rockefeller Foundation in 1956 and 1957 made two grants to finance the NPA Project on the Economics of Competitive Coexistence. The Foundation is not, however, to be understood as approving by virtue of its grants any of the views expressed in research studies growing out of the project.

NPA is grateful for the Rockefeller Foundation's financial support and is deeply indebted to all who are contributing to this Project: to the chairman and the members of the Special Project Committee on the Economics of Competitive Coexistence; to the Project's research staff; and especially to Mr. Alec Nove, the author of the present study on Communist Economic Strategy: Soviet Growth and Capabilities.

H. Christian Sonne
Chairman, NPA Board of Trustees

v

STATEMENT

by the

NPA Special Project Committee on THE ECONOMICS OF COMPETITIVE
COEXISTENCE

This study, the third devoted to communist economic strategy, deals
with the Soviet Union in its role as the originator and the nerve center
of the contest that has been called "competitive coexistence." The Soviet
Union's central position in the Communist bloc rests not only on its historical
and political primacy; it arises, as well, from its ability to assist others--
within the bloc and among the uncommitted countries--with the wherewithal
of economic development, credits, and capital goods. In the years since
Stalin's death, the bloc, with the USSR as its spokesman and leader, has
made its weight felt in the world economy in an increasing number of
ways: as a provider of capital and technical assistance; as a buyer of surpluses and an aggressive seller of other commodities in Western markets;
and, with particular stress on the aspirations of the less developed areas,
as the self-styled champion of rapid industrialization. The future Soviet
capabilities in these fields are the core of the present study. It is expedient
to view them in conjunction, for they are interdependent.

More trade is apt to accompany Soviet development at the stage when
industrialization has enhanced both the capacity to absorb more primary
products and to supply more manufactures, especially capital goods for
development abroad. In Stalin's time an extreme policy of isolation and
autarky kept Soviet trade at an abnormally low level. There is no indication
of an intent to let the Soviet bloc become overly dependent on trade with
the noncommunist world in the future. But as the bloc economies grow,
there is ample scope for a sizable expansion even though Soviet trade is
unlikely to become very large in terms of world totals. While trade
will always be marginal for the continent-sized economy of the USSR,
it is quite important for East-Central Europe; and Communist China,
which cannot do without imported equipment and material, has to export
to finance such purchases.

In fact, Soviet-bloc exports are developing into a disturbing element
in world trade. Textiles and other consumer goods from Mainland China,
priced to sell against any competition, are making inroads into Japan's
markets in Southeast Asia. Chinese tin, re-exported by the Soviet Union,
has hit Western markets in a period of flagging demand. Russian exports
of aluminum, lead, and zinc have also aggravated vulnerable markets.
Even though Soviet consent appears to have been secured for a temporary
reduction of these exports, it has become evident that future bloc capacity
for more trade, possibly for seriously disrupting trade, may greatly exceed
the present still modest level.

At the same time, under the pressure of growth requirements on limited
resources, the bloc has proved a willing buyer from primary-producing

countries with surpluses of products the West cannot absorb. The opportunity of exchanging redundant commodities against essentials for consumption and development does not lack attraction even for those who would prefer cash to barter; and while some countries have become aware of snags in bilateral deals, the lure of Sino-Soviet trade is apt to become more effective with every failure to mitigate the instability of Western commodity markets. Moreover, in times of recession, the Soviet markets for capital goods can hardly fail to offer more attraction to Western producers.

Soviet capacity for foreign aid has been enhanced by rapid growth at home. In fact, in spite of a thumping propaganda campaign, rather artlessly underlined by excessive Western anxiety, Soviet aid deliveries have not been large. But in terms of aggregate income and investment they could undoubtedly be stepped up considerably if attractive targets would be found. Moreover, most bloc assistance takes the form of credits repayable in local products and are not an unmitigated sacrifice, except temporarily.

So far Soviet aid has been selective, but overall capacity would hardly stand in the way of a much broader program in the uncommitted areas. The bloc's own calls on limited productive facilities do impose a limit on such activities, though there is no doubt that whenever political strategy seems to require it, sufficient resources can always be mustered to swamp any small country. But the growing demands for China's industrialization and the equipment of East-Central Europe for coordinated bloc growth would inevitably compete with a very large increase of Soviet foreign aid.

It would be futile to discuss bloc capabilities without reference to the Soviet Union's own growth prospects. A rapidly increasing output clearly enhances the potential for all kinds of action. But growth itself requires very large resources and the Soviet economy has long been laboring under the strain of forced draft. With future advance depending relatively more on rising productivity than on the growth of the labor force, a period of great effort and much institutional experimentation lies ahead. Even though the seven-year plan 1959/65 calls for a somewhat reduced percentage growth of output, the demands on human and financial resources are great; they seem to leave little margin for large activities outside the bloc, except at the expense of the Soviet consumer whose demands the planners find ever harder to resist.

This concentration on the domestic task of Soviet growth is not, by the same token, without political value abroad. On the contrary, the Soviet example of rapid industrialization is ceaselessly propounded as the only fast and sure road to economic development and power for poor areas. This particular demonstration of tangible advance has a powerful appeal to some leaders, reformers and impatient young intellectuals in the new nations. It may well prove to be as potent a Soviet weapon as the magnitude of trade and aid.

It is in terms of growth that the Soviet leaders have stated their ultimate challenge to the West. International comparisons of growth are controversial and there is no unanimity about the precise rate of Soviet growth; yet currently it is undeniably higher than that of most countries in the West, even if not as fast as the Soviets claim. Though their claim of surpassing the United States in overall or per capita production within the next 10 to

15 years is vastly exaggerated, the very ability to throw out such a challenge is evidence of a new self-confidence and economic vigor which cannot fail to impress uncommitted nations that lack both. And even in the West, this display of resolve and purpose had better be viewed as a potential challenge of formidable and growing proportions.

The NPA Special Project Committee on the Economics of Competitive Coexistence believes that the study Communist Economic Strategy: Soviet Growth and Capabilities by Alec Nove is a valuable and timely contribution in a period of change and stress in the Soviet Union. Without endorsing details for which the author, in collaboration with the Director of Research, assumes responsibility, and without subscribing necessarily to all inter-pretations and policy implications suggested by the study, the Committee recommends publication of this study to the NPA Board of Trustees.

Members of the NPA Special Project Committee
on THE ECONOMICS OF COMPETITIVE COEXISTENCE
Signing the Statement

SIMON KUZNETS (Chairman)
Professor of Political Economy
Johns Hopkins University

JOHN H. ADLER
Economic Advisor
International Bank for
Reconstruction and Development

FRANK ALTSCHUL
Chairman of the Board
General American
Investors Company

SOLOMON BARKIN
Director of Research
Textile Workers Union
of America, AFL-CIO

AUGUST HECKSCHER
Director
The Twentieth Century Fund

II. STRUVE HENSEL
Attorney
Washington, D. C.

MAX F. MILLIKAN
Director
Center for International
Studies
Massachusetts Institute
of Technology

ARTHUR MOORE
The Washington Bureau
McGraw-Hill Publications

PHILIP E. MOSELY
Director of Studies
Council on Foreign Relations

PAUL H. NITZE
President
Foreign Service
Educational Foundation

H. CHRISTIAN SONNE
President
South Ridge Corporation

FOREWORD

This study of Soviet capabilities was preceded by two other reports in a series on Communist Economic Strategy. The first dealt with East-Central Europe, a region that has vastly grown in importance within the Soviet bloc, as a provider of specialized equipment to the Soviet Union and as a nucleus of trade with the uncommitted countries. The second report pictured the rise of Communist China which is devising its own ruthless method for a rapid growth of its economic and political power. But the Soviet Union is the first in time and still, despite Chinese self-assertion, the first in rank within the Communist bloc; therefore the present study evaluates the potentialities of the Soviet Union for economic growth, for trade and aid.

Much has happened in the Soviet Union since Stalin's death. Khrushchev's emergence as the maker of policy was not uncontested. But he has proved to be a bold innovator, attempting to improve productivity by unprecedented reforms in agriculture, industry, and education. He is clearly aware that the future rate of progress depends upon greater efficiency based on technological and institutional change; and, recognizing the temper of the times and the mood of the people who must push the economy up the ladder of efficiency, he has had to rely more on incentives to the producer and more promises to the consumer.

This, in terms of limited resources, is bound to be costly. It also calls for more experiments, with all the economic and political risk this involves in the rigid pattern of totalitarian societies where change tends to take the form of jerky drives instead of smooth evolution. If it succeeds, it is hard to foretell its shape and appraise the outcome. If it fails, the rate of growth would be affected. It is, therefore, singularly difficult to evaluate the impact of changes which are still unfolding before our eyes.

Yet, one cannot fail to recognize the capability of the Soviet system to grow at a high rate, if not as rapidly as it is claimed. Even a somewhat declining rate of growth, as forecast by some observers, would mean rapidly increasing yearly increments of output which, in some sectors, are already nearing those of the United States, though total Soviet output still lags far behind. Moreover, as a very high proportion of this increment is plowed back with single-minded determination into those economic sectors that produce more military or civilian growth potential, more capacity for foreign assistance, or a combination of these, the impetus of the forward movement is compounded. It would be futile to look for comfort to the absolute magnitudes while closing one's eyes to the dynamic force which is already capturing the attention, sometimes the admiration, of the poorer nations, whose hopes for substantive advancement rest on very high rates of growth.

In this time of experimentation and transformation of the Soviet economy one needs a nimble brush to paint a picture in a few bold strokes. Detailed studies have been written by Soviet experts on many complex aspects of the bloc economy. By contrast, the author of the present study was asked to write an essay that passes over the detail in favor of a broad impression and a closely reasoned evaluation of Soviet growth and capabilities. The NPA Project on the Economics of Competitive Coexistence was fortunate to find in Mr. Alec Nove an expert who was willing to undertake this uncommon task. Mr. Nove was born in Russia and educated in England where he studied at the London School of Economics. After war service in the British Army he held a number of civil service positions and is now a Reader in Russian social and economic studies at the University of London. He has visited the Soviet Union repeatedly over the past years and is the author of numerous articles on the Soviet economy.

In addition to the untiring assistance of Dr. Gerhard Colm, NPA Chief Economist, the project staff and the author are indebted to Abram Bergson, Joseph Berliner, Herbert Block, Robert W. Campbell, David Granick, Gregory Grossman, Leon Herman, Hans Heymann, Oleg Hoeffding, Franklyn D. Holzman, Holland Hunter, Naum Jasny, Michael Kaser, G. Warren Nutter, Raymond P. Powell, Francis Seton, Nicolas Spulber, Paul Wohl, Jan Wszelaki and Alfred Zauberman for extensive comments and criticism of an earlier version of the manuscript. This acknowledgment is, however, not intended to imply any responsibility of such persons for the conclusions or opinions expressed by the author of this study.

With few exceptions, only data and information available to the writer by May 31, 1959, could be considered in this study. In a field where developments sometimes follow each other in rapid sequence, this cautionary note seems well worth bearing in mind.

Henry G. Aubrey, Director of Research
The Economics of Competitive Coexistence

COMMUNIST ECONOMIC STRATEGY:
SOVIET GROWTH AND CAPABILITIES

by

Alec Nove

INTRODUCTION

The object of this paper is to consider the probable effectiveness of the Soviet bloc's effort to win the battle of "peaceful coexistence." The subject is a vast one, and it is obviously impossible to do justice to every aspect of the many problems involved. The intention is to present a necessarily very general survey of the various factors bearing on competitive capability. At the center of the analysis will be the heart and leader of the bloc, the USSR, though attention will also be devoted to other countries in the Soviet orbit, so as to take into account the USSR's position within the bloc and to help evaluate its overall capabilities.

Since the assumptions on which the study is based preclude a direct military clash, the effectiveness of the Soviet effort will be measured by its success or otherwise in winning over the uncommitted world, notably the so-called underdeveloped countries. The impact of the Soviet bloc on these countries operates at a number of different levels. The purely political level--notably crude subversion--is beyond the scope of this paper, which will concentrate on economic aspects of the struggle. Naturally, the political atmosphere is most relevant to the effectiveness of various economic moves. Thus, as has been so well shown by Dr. Berliner,[1]/ the anti-imperialist myth surrounding the USSR has greatly contributed to the political publicity value of relatively small offers of aid. It is also important to note that the economic progress of the Soviet bloc has great effects even in the absence of any appreciable trade or aid activities. For example, India's trading relationships remain (and surely will remain) dominated by Western countries; yet the impact of the USSR and China on Indian minds is a vital and potentially very dangerous factor. A mental climate in which the Soviet methods of doing things are accepted as right and successful would greatly facilitate the overthrow of pro-Western regimes. Nor should one neglect the effect of the build-up of Soviet economic power on the military potential of the bloc, which, even if it is not in fact used, has already had a profound psychological effect on the underdeveloped world.

These indirect effects of Soviet growth are sometimes neglected, and instead the immediate economic drives of the bloc in underdeveloped countries are dramatized. The existence of political dangers arising from direct Soviet "economic intervention" is a fact, and so the probable development of economic relations between the bloc and these countries must be given due consideration. Yet, on a longer-term view, the building up

---

Note: All footnotes appear on pages 75-79.

1

of the internal economic might of the bloc may be the decisive factor. On the available evidence, this is the view of the Soviet leaders, and planning is based on this line of thinking. Khrushchev evidently believes that the uncommitted countries must naturally gravitate toward the Soviet way when the USSR and its allies are capable of outproducing the western world, and are more efficient than America. It is also evident that an economically mighty bloc will be far better equipped to supply the needs of the underdeveloped world, to outbid the West, and to disorganize the "capitalist" markets at will. It is unlikely that Khrushchev overlooks these considerations, even while he is concentrating his energies and the bloc's resources primarily on internal growth.

Because of the key role of the economic build-up within the bloc in any forward look, much of this paper will be devoted to examining the various factors affecting economic growth in the near future. These factors will be considered under the following headings:

1. The Will. This means the determination of the rulers of the Soviet world to pursue the aim of intersystem competition, and their willingness or ability to give all out priority to it. This involves some assessment of the social pressures which are now emerging.

2. Resources. It is necessary briefly to consider how far the availability and accessibility of materials, and the potential of the labor force affect the situation, and also to refer to the vast investment problems which must arise.

3. Organization. One must deal with such vital questions as the ability of the Soviet system to use resources efficiently. Granted its "success" in imposing sacrifices to build heavy industry by autocratic methods, can the system now adapt itself to the very different and more flexible needs of a modern industrial state? Must agriculture be the "Achilles' heel" of the economy? Because Soviet influence in the underdeveloped world largely stems from the belief that Soviet methods are effective, these matters affect the impact of Sovietism, as well as being relevant to the process of growth within the bloc.

After discussing these aspects of the internal scene, and drawing a few necessarily very general conclusions about the future pace of economic development, we shall turn to the bloc's impact on the underdeveloped world, its force of example as a model to follow, its ability to give economic aid, and the likely growth of its trading relations with the outside world. An important point which must be emphasized is the distinction between capability and the actual priorities in the disposal of resources. For example, it is easy to establish that the USSR or Czechoslovakia could, if the appropriate decisions were taken, greatly expand their exports or credits to one or more countries very quickly. It is also beyond doubt that the ability of bloc countries to do these things will increase rapidly with the continued progress of economic expansion. But it does not follow that this will actually be done, for resources may be tied up in ambitious projects within the Soviet world. Therefore, our conclusions must be related to a necessarily somewhat speculative estimate of intention. We must, among other things, take into account the tendency to avoid excessive dependence on trade with the outside world, the preferences of planners for autarky, and the priority which may be given by bloc countries to each others' needs.

The paper will from time to time seek to generalize about the bloc as a whole. Yet, in quite essential matters, the bloc is anything but a single unit. It includes highly developed industrial communities like East Germany and Czechoslovakia; poor and backward Bulgaria; and politically explosive Poland and Hungary, where every economic step must be carefully adjusted to avoid upsetting the precarious grip of the regime on an actively discontented people. The USSR, since Stalin's death, is undergoing internal changes, the full consequences of which cannot yet be estimated. Mainland China, obviously a great industrial power in the long run, is at an early stage of industrialization, with all the acute social-economic problems associated with this painful process.

It is evident that few generalizations can apply to so varied a group, the more so as small efforts are now made to impose a uniform pattern of economic development. Yet in endeavoring to study the capabilities of the bloc as a whole, it will be necessary to some extent to abstract from the peculiarities of this or that country. The USSR, as the senior and most powerful member, will receive the most attention, but it will be necessary repeatedly to point to differences between her and other bloc countries.

Chapter One

POLITICAL AND SOCIAL FACTORS -- THE WILL AND THE DRIVE

THE DYNAMICS OF EXPANSIONISM

The rulers of the Soviet bloc are endeavoring to catch up with the Western world in economic might. They have imposed heavy sacrifices on its peoples in pursuit of this aim, and have neglected a large number of projects which, while desirable in themselves, compete for resources with the overriding purpose of maximizing growth. We should not go so far as to attribute the industrialization of Russia wholly to the Communists, since the process would have gone on (albeit probably at a reduced pace and in different directions) without them. It is also clear that the industrialization of China was held back by anarchy and war, and would have inevitably followed the establishment of order under almost any conceivable government.

Nonetheless, no one can seriously doubt that the rapidity of industrial development, and its peculiar challenge to the West, are directly connected with the ideological beliefs of the Soviet leaders and their ability to impose the priority of growth on their subjects. The same beliefs impel them toward regarding their economic programs as an integral part of the ultimate conflict between East and West. Here again, it is desirable to avoid the extreme view which seeks a directly "political" explanation for every Soviet economic decision. Thus the 1958 decree on the output of plastics is explicable in purely economic terms, despite its origin in a decision of the central committee of the Communist party, and the sale of aluminum in world markets in 1958 was more probably motivated by a desire to earn foreign currency than by a sinister intention to disorganize a falling market.

Yet the ultimate object of economic policy as a whole, the source of its dynamics, is political-ideological. Therefore, any change in the political-ideological balance must have its effect on economic growth and so on the challenge which we have to face. Has such a change occurred? Is it possible? Can we reasonably project the trends of the past into the indefinite future? These would seem to be vital questions.

For some critics, these questions may seem pointless. They may argue that the purposes of policy can be assumed to be unchanging, that only tactics and current maneuvers vary. While this is not the place to discuss the ultimate aims of Communism, it would seem -- from what has already occurred -- that a very considerable "dilution" of the effective priorities in the economic field can take place, without any major change in either basic ideology or in the political character of the regime. In looking at the competitive capabilities of the Soviet bloc, the degree of belief of the Soviet leaders in the ultimate triumph of Communism is hardly very relevant. It is what they do that matters. It is therefore desirable briefly to examine the various factors involved in the dynamics of economic expansion.

The factors which must be taken into account include: Communist ideology, fear of enemies (real or supposed), power-seeking, nationalism, and also the relationship between rulers and ruled. Each of these is affected by social and political change, and by the eroding effects of time. For, it may be asked, why, forty years after the Russian Revolution, should we expect the original messianic beliefs to retain their grip on the Soviet leadership? Should not they, and the ruling group as a whole, come to take a less combative view of their task, to see the virtues of stability, order, security? Whatever may be the personal beliefs of Khrushchev, will time not weaken the ideological element in Soviet dynamism? One cannot presume to answer the question, which, in any case, will never be posed in quite this way or in isolation from other relevant factors. Yet it should never be wholly overlooked.

One of the essential "stimulants" to Soviet dynamism is fear. Tension provides the party with an excuse to maintain discipline, and fear of superior economic power of potential enemies is one of the impulses behind the economic race. Its political value has been so great that it has at times been engineered. A particularly good example of "artificial" fear was the nonsense about "intervention" by Chamberlain and Poincaré which was publicized in Russia around 1929. Nonetheless, it would be wrong not to see that there are also some genuinely-held fears, and to this extent our own actions are relevant; we can "contribute" to Soviet dynamism by the degree of our hostility. The cold war is a vital part of the picture not only in the Soviet Union but in China, where a drastic speedup in industrialization has been decreed, and in Poland, where fear of Germany contributes to maintaining the regime in being. It may be, of course, that for this very reason the Soviet leaders will ensure that the cold war remains with us.

However, there are also internal enemies, and this brings one on to the "power-seeking" motive. It is frequently asserted that ideology must be maintained in its pure militant form, because it provides the raison d'être of party power. There is some truth in this, although the protagonists of this view should remember that the practical content of ideology can change appreciably without endangering this monopoly. More, the power position of the regime depends in part on its being able to identify itself with dynamic elements in society, on being able to legitimize itself in the minds of people by performing some function which is widely regarded as "necessary." This compels some adjustment of policy to social pressure (of which more will be said), as part of the price of maintaining the power position intact.

The role of terror in this context is widely misunderstood. It was very largely of negative value -- it suppressed opposition, and made possible rapid capital accumulation by the imposition of sacrifices. While it certainly facilitated through forced labor, as a by-product of mass arrests, the development of remote and inhospitable regions, the immense economic waste -- including the killing off of scarce technicians and administrators -- make it (in my view) absurd to assert that the material achievements of the Soviet regime were directly attributable to terror and forced labor. Thus it is no coincidence that the economic sector in which coercion played the greatest role -- collective agriculture -- remained the most backward; orders unrelated to self-interest could not be translated into effective action. 1/ In any event, few can doubt that the complex and increasingly educated Soviet society of today cannot function efficiently without a much greater degree of voluntary cooperation "below." The post-Stalin period in the USSR has been characterized by efforts to find some way of reconciling the political power of the party with the need to secure more active participation among the citizens. The interpretation which insists on "pure totalitarian power" cannot explain the major concessions which have in fact been made.

This is in part a consequence of technical progress. To take a military parallel: The army of Frederick the Great could have been organized on the basis of the soldiers being "more frightened of their officers than of the enemy." However, the development of military technique gradually made it impossible to base an army on such a principle and demanded the use of initiative among the junior ranks. Or, to use a more directly relevant example: Forced labor could be used to build the railroad to the arctic coal mines of Vorkuta, but the effective operation of the railroad requires a different relationship between incentives and coercion. These factors have to be taken into account by the Soviet leaders, however totalitarian their philosophy or their intentions, because otherwise the race with the West cannot be effectively run. The end, in the Soviet Union, of a period of relative abundance of labor, with the consequent rise in the relative importance of productivity per head, reinforces the importance of incentives.

Like all generalizations, this one should not be pressed too far. Stalin was well aware of the advantages of incentives, and used them, along with coercion, to stimulate effort, even in the forced-labor camps themselves. Nor has coercion disappeared under his successors. However, it remains true that, in the USSR and in many of her European satellites, an important shift is visible in the balance between incentives and coercion. The director who fails to do his job, the worker who walks out, are now penalized through their pocketbooks and not through the criminal law.

China, however, is in quite a different position, for a number of reasons. First, the regime has been in power for only a relatively few years, and so the initial dynamism, the will to change society, is still fresh. Second, the basic process of social revolution, which was largely completed in the Soviet Union in the early thirties, is still very much to the forefront in China, involving the constant use of coercion. Far from showing any signs of a "softer" attitude toward its citizens, the Chinese Communists are more demanding, more ruthless, less concerned with comfort and with stability. The contrast with the USSR in this respect has struck every acute observer. China's period of "primitive accumulation" is in full swing. The USSR has moved on to a later stage in its development. Finally, there is some evidence to suggest that China's people are more obedient, can be made to work harder, can be pushed around to a greater extent, than the Russians were even by Stalin. It may be that nationalism plays a major role here. By this is meant not only national tradition, but also the support which the Chinese Communists may derive from being the first within living memory to enforce order and assert national authority in the world arena. Perhaps even more than in the USSR, national pride has played a big role in mobilizing effort for industrialization.

We must note the very different role of nationalism elsewhere in the bloc. While in the USSR and China it acts (on the whole) as an ally of the regime and as a dynamic force, in Poland, Hungary, or Rumania it plays the

6

opposite role. The anti-Soviet, anti-Russian national traditions of these countries and the resentment at having to follow policies decided abroad -- these things are obstacles to rapid development, and the outbreaks in Poland and Hungary led to a cut in investment in heavy industry and a reduced rate of growth.

EFFECTS OF SOCIAL PRESSURES

The practical relevance of all these considerations to the competitive capability of the bloc lies in their effect on growth rates, and in raising questions about the stability of the regime and cohesion within the bloc. The ability to neglect the needs of citizens is one of the factors which has raised the "growth-effectiveness" of investment well above Western levels. By this is meant the tendency to devote a higher proportion of productive capacity, and of investment resources, to the generation of more production rather than for the provision of consumable goods and services. Thus, the bulk of investment in transportation was designed to serve industry rather than people; the bulk of building materials was directed to factory-building; and hardly any foreign currency was used to buy consumers' goods.

However, in the USSR (but not in China) there have been big changes, which must have a major effect on the utilization of resources. The incomes of peasants have been raised; there has been a sharp rise in pensions; heavy investments have been made in food production; the rate of house building is being doubled; hours of labor have been reduced; it is no longer an offense to change one's job without permission; and efforts are being made to improve amenities, especially in rural areas. The list could be prolonged. The Soviet seven-year plan (1959-65) abounds in promises to continue this trend: still shorter hours, higher minimum wages, more pensions, a big housing drive, much emphasis on improved diet, and a much increased effort to re-equip the light and food industries. A similar trend toward paying more attention to the consumer is visible in several of the European satellites. The effect has been to divert resources from growth-inducing sectors. Scarce materials and labor are being diverted to house-building, and investments in heavy industry have inevitably been affected.

In looking ahead, it is relevant to point out that these concessions have not been accompanied by any weakening of the party's grip on political power. It can be argued that the concessions were due to the temporary absence of a dictator after Stalin's death, and that, now that Khrushchev is firmly in the saddle, what has been given can be taken away. However, such a view seems to disregard certain practical problems, of which Khrushchev is evidently acutely conscious. The factors which have already been referred to, and which have tilted the balance between coercion and incentives toward greater reliance on incentives, do not hinge on the existence or non-existence of a supreme dictator in the Kremlin. It remains as true as ever that increased agricultural production demands better and more assured pay and improved amenities; that it is extremely important to stimulate higher productivity by offering rewards and encouraging initiative; that the upper crust in Soviet society cannot be denied some satisfaction of their growing demands for private automobiles, hotels, better living, demands which have been stimulated by their greater awareness of standards of life abroad.

The need to develop new regions, in conditions where mass forced labor is no longer present, necessarily calls for inducements, including tolerable housing. An example of this may be found in the investment figures in the Vorkuta coal field area in the Arctic, which was formerly worked by forced labor and to which it is now necessary to attract workers (the author has seen "Come to Vorkuta" advertisements on notice boards in Leningrad and elsewhere). It has been found necessary, in consequence, to devote half of the investments in the Vorkuta coal field to housing. 2/ All this means that a smaller proportion of investments will directly "generate" additional production. Such trends can hardly be reversed by ordering the chief of the secret police to imprison or shoot some malcontents. Khrushchev's recent policies suggest that he is taking these factors into account in framing his internal policies and does not propose to go back in these respects toward Stalinist practices. The extensive concessions embodied in the seven-year plan (1959-65) are fully consistent with this interpretation.

Thus a positive response to social pressures seems an inevitable feature of Soviet reality at present and in the foreseeable future. To this extent, the policies of the ruling party show a change in practical priorities, a change which must tend to diminish somewhat the pace of growth (except where, as in China, a different situation prevails). This is not to suggest that the ultimate aims of the leadership have withered away. To Khrushchev and his colleagues, the concessions which have been made are part of the search for the most effective way of pursuing the aim of overtaking the West and winning the support of the uncommitted world. It may be useful to imagine an optimum rate of growth, achieved by combined inputs of persuasion and coercion. The proportions in which these are combined vary at different times and places, and it would seem that some substitution of persuasion for coercion has been a condition for achieving the highest practicable growth rate in the present circumstances. But the effect is still to diminish the share of the national income directly devoted to the running of the race.

Chapter Two

RESOURCES FOR ECONOMIC COMPETITION

INTRODUCTION

This section will be concerned with resources of materials and man-power; the problems of so utilizing the available resources as to permit rapid growth; and the problems which affect the "growth-effectiveness" of investment. Each of the matters treated could easily be the subject of a separate report, or even a sizable book, so in the nature of things only the barest survey can be attempted here.

MATERIAL RESOURCES FOR INDUSTRY

The USSR is aiming to "overtake America" within fifteen years in aggregate industrial production, and the data of Table 1 have been given publicity and presented as an attainable minimum.

Table 1

Selected Soviet Commodity Targets, 1965 and 1972

	Unit	1957	1958	1965 Plan a/ Targets	1972 Plan a/ Targets
Iron ore	(mill. tons)	84.2	88.8	155	275
Coal	(mill. tons)	463.4	496	603	700
Oil	(mill. tons)	98.3	113	235	375
Pig iron	(mill. tons)	37.0	39.6	67.5	80
Steel	(mill. tons)	51.1	54.9	88.5	110
Electricity	(bill. kwh)	209.5	233	510	850
Natural gas	(bill.cub.met.)	20.2	29.8	150	235
Cement	(mill. tons)	28.9	33.3	78	100
Wool cloth	(mill. meters)	282.1	303	500	600
Leather					
footwear	(mill. pairs)	315	356	515	650
Sugar	(mill. tons)	4.5	5.4	9.6	9.5b/

a/ Mid-point of range.
b/ In the case of sugar, the 1972 estimate is evidently due for upward amendment.
Source: Pravda, Moscow, January 16, 1957, November 7, 1958.
Note: For fuller details of the 1965 plan, see Appendix Table 2.

The 1972 plan figures were announced in the anniversary speech on the fortieth birthday of the Russian revolution, and certainly do not represent anything firm or final. Indeed, comparison of the 1972 commodity targets with those subsequently published for 1965 suggest that the former would now be extensively revised, principally in an upward direction.

China was aiming to surpass the industrial output of Great Britain within the same period, but the much more rapid growth of 1958 suggests that this is now expected to be achieved much earlier. The long-term plans of the European satellites are still not quite clear, but all envisage ambitious growth tempos. We must briefly consider how far material shortages are likely to hold back the rate of progress.

There have been a number of admirable studies of various aspects of this question. 1/ Since their publication, a number of valuable mineral discoveries have been made, which give some promise of relief to the shortages foreseen by the authors of these studies. Nonetheless, difficulties will evidently persist. Thus, while iron ore is available in large quantities in the Kursk-Belgorod area and in Asia (Kustanai and East Siberia), the ore is of lower grade than that previously available both in the Krivoi Rog and the Urals areas, and requires additional investment in ore concentration plants. The physical output targets for iron ore appear to be attainable, but the conversion of this ore into iron and steel is bound to cause strains and bottlenecks.

The most obvious and immediate of these obstacles is coking coal. This is in short supply, except in areas remote from existing or projected centers of the steel industry, for example the Pechora basin (Vorkuta). It is intended to use Kuzbas coking coal in the new East Siberian metallurgical center of Taishet, which again means a long overland haul, though vigorous prospecting is going on to find alternative sources. A particularly bad example of uneconomic siting of an existing steelworks is Cherepovets, in the Vologda oblast. Ore is transported 1,500 kilometers, coking coal (from Vorkuta) 1,900 kilometers, and costs are understandably said to be very high. 2/

All this does not mean that the ferrous metallurgy goals cannot be reached. It does, however, suggest that the cost of meeting them will be high, which, in turn, will require a disproportionate diversion of scarce resources.

Table 2 illustrates the big change which is planned in the make up of the Soviet fuel balance.

There appear to be ample supplies of relatively low-cost oil and natural gas, the use of which will relieve the heavy strain of long coal hauls on the railways. The development of pipelines is being energetically pressed forward, 3/ and there are remarkable advances in the transmission of power over long distances to the power-deficient central area of Russia.

Soviet economists have been stressing of late the relative backwardness of the USSR in energy production per head, borne out in a calculation by Academician Nemchinov for the year 1956, shown in Table 3. He emphasized that the quantity envisaged for 1965 would still leave the Soviet Union well behind the United Kingdom. However, there is no suggestion of an

Table 2

Soviet Fuel Balance, 1957 and Planned 1972
(Percent)

	1957	1972 Plan
Coal	60.8	32.2
Oil	23.4	34.4
Natural gas	4.0	23.3
Peat	3.8	2.4
Hydroelectricity	2.9	2.6
Atomic energy	-	3.2
Firewood	4.4	1.3
Shale	0.7	0.6

Source: Sokolova, Voprosy Ekonomiki, No. 5/1958, p. 65.

Table 3

Energy Production--Soviet Estimate
for USSR and West, 1956
(Coal equivalent per capita in tons)

United States	8.58
United Kingdom	5.03
Western Europe	2.68
USSR	2.45

Source: Kommunist, No. 1/1959, p. 83.

overall energy shortage in relation to the requirements of the plan, and analyses by fuel experts have tended to concentrate rather on the problem of the possible extent of Soviet exportable surpluses of oil. It also seems probable that the necessary materials exist for the large expansion, envisaged by the plan, of the petrochemical industry, although the sheer pace demanded by the plan (trebling the entire chemical industry in seven years) may well cause acute strains and bottlenecks.

It is essential to note that much of the USSR has not yet been properly surveyed. "So far as I can tell," wrote Shimkin, "no major area of the Soviet Union has yet been subjected to thorough geological study....Present knowledge appears to grade from rough economic assessment to complete ignorance." 4/ His views find confirmation in the recent discoveries of Soviet prospectors, of which the diamond field in the Yakutsk area is one. If this is the case in the Soviet Union, how much more does it apply to China, especially to its more remote provinces? We must expect many more rich discoveries to be made, though of course it is impossible to forecast what they will be. It is worth recalling that, for example, the

11

expansion in recent years of U.S. oil production would have surprised the oil experts of 25 years ago--yet America had been fairly thoroughly surveyed.

Judging from recently published trade statistics, the USSR still relies heavily on imports of certain "metal ores" (probably largely uranium) and nonferrous metals, but much of these can now be imported from within the bloc. Thus the "anonymous" metal ores come largely from China and Czechoslovakia, while tin import needs are more than satisfied by China, and copper remains in deficit. But the rapid expansion of the chemical industry, and of plastics and synthetics, should further diminish the dependence on the bloc on essential imports. The necessary materials exist, especially in the USSR, in ample quantities.

There remain a large number of commodities of varying degrees of essentiality, which the bloc will tend to import, and these will be discussed in due course. However, on the evidence before us, it does no seem likely that the ambitious growth plans will be limited by problems of sheer physical availability of resources to carry them out.

Of course, physical availability is only part of the story. Location raises some extremely awkward problems. Many of the vital minerals are to be found in areas lacking transportation facilities and remote from centers of industry and population. This raises questions of the future returns to investment, which will be further considered below. It also particularly affects the situation of the European satellites. Some of these countries are deficient in minerals and fuel, and have so far tended to build much of their heavy industry on imports from the USSR. Thus, almost 11 million tons of Soviet iron ore were exported to the satellites in 1957, as well as over 7.5 million tons of coal and, judging from present plans, these figures will increase further. This requires very long hauls, and is generally quite uneconomic.

Such enterprises as the steel works at Sztalinvaros, Hungary, must be a heavy burden to the economy and their very existence is a monument to the triumph of politically inspired irrationality over economic common sense. There are signs that this is understood by bloc planners. Thus the Czechs and the Hungarians have been giving public expression to the view that, in their situation, industries requiring a relatively heavy weight of metal are best avoided. Long and expensive transportation of fuel may be to some extent reduced by the extension of Soviet oil and gas pipelines into satellite territories. There is much talk of a more intelligent specialization. Since there is not much likelihood of any large undiscovered mineral resources in Czechoslovakia, Poland, or Hungary, it follows that there will develop a tendency toward more modest plans for expanding steel output, and more emphasis on machinery, especially machinery requiring less metal and more human skill and precision.

In so far as growth in the USSR has been due to the utilization of readily available and unused natural resources, "Soviet" tempos of growth seem to be beyond the satellites' powers. However, the build-up of a big machinery industry in these countries will be of value to the USSR and China as importers, and must also be expected to lead to increasingly competitive selling in underdeveloped countries.

The situation is much less favorable when one turns to agriculture. Despite the vast size of its land mass, the bloc's usable farmland is severely limited by permafrost, bog, forest, and desert. Bringing new land under cultivation by irrigation or clearance is a necessarily costly and slow business. Most of the good quality soils, especially in the USSR, are in areas which are deficient in rainfall, and so there are big year-by-year variations in the harvests. The great effort made since 1954 to expand cultivation in the marginal steppelands of Asia cannot be repeated, and indeed the necessities of soil conservation are likely to lead to a slight fall in the total sown area. Thus, looking ahead, it is impossible to see any aggregate increase in the area under cultivation in the USSR. There is no agricultural equivalent of building new factories. Nor can anyone take seriously the panaceas -- such as the "plan for the transformation of nature" -- which were so dear to Soviet propagandists in Stalin's time.

While the European satellites certainly have no chance of expanding the area under cultivation, the case of China requires careful consideration. The remarkably good 1958 harvest, according to Peking's claims, 5/ was due not to the favorable weather but to a number of measures which could have a durable effect: the expansion of the sown area in the north; a tremendous expansion in irrigation, affecting (if official sources are to be believed) 28 million hectares or 70 million acres in this one year 1958; a big increase in double cropping; deeper ploughing; and more use of fertilizer. It is, of course, impossible to assess the success of agricultural policies on the basis of one good year. Both the soil and the peasantry have been heavily burdened, the latter having also to shoulder the tasks of rural industrialization. It is altogether too soon to say whether a durable "forward leap" has been achieved in agriculture.

That there is much scope for improvement may been seen by a comparison between yields per hectare in China and the much higher yields achieved annually in the intensively cultivated peasant holdings in Japan. Much depends on whether the intensity of cultivation achieved by private peasants on small holdings in Japan can be reproduced on large collectives or communes in China. Soviet experience will be of little use in this connection, as Soviet collective and state farms have hitherto been most successful (or least unsuccessful) in coping with large-scale extensive cultivation. On China, therefore, it seems prudent to reserve judgment, neither accepting the official story in full nor obstinately refusing to recognize the possibility of very considerable gains. Official plans, however, inspired by the 1958 claims, seem to have quite lost touch with reality, envisaging tremendous increases from year to year.

The USSR is also planning very substantial advances. The 1965 targets are given in detail in Appendix Table 3, and these may be compared with official figures (or reasonably reliable estimates) of recent performance. It is noteworthy that the major myths of past plans have been modified. Thus the grain harvest target for 1960 (180 million tons) has been converted into the less fantastic "10 to 11 milliard poods" (164-180 million tons) in 1965. The greatly publicized campaign of multiplying Soviet meat output three and a half fold, to exceed U.S. per capita production by 1961, has been quietly dropped. This implied 21 million tons, but the new target for 1965 is "only" 16 million tons. All this represents overdue signs of sanity, but remains extremely ambitious. A 70 percent increase in farm output in the seven years is aimed at. Since the cultivated area cannot be significantly increased, this would call for great intensification of agriculture.

Organizational weaknesses which stand in the way of intensification, and of rational use of land and labor, will be discussed in greater detail in the next chapter. At this stage it is sufficient to emphasize the undoubted possibility of organizational improvements; the series of agricultural reforms in the USSR in recent years, culminating in the elimination of the Machine Tractor Stations and the establishment of a single price system in 1958, affords evidence that the attempt is at any rate being made. Many of the weaknesses of the past were directly connected with the exploitation of agriculture for the benefit of industrial growth (there is a direct connection between low farm prices and compulsion, and between compulsion and inefficiency); therefore the price increases which have been granted6/ must be expected to improve the quality of work done.

However, all the above relates principally to the USSR. The satellites are in a very different position, since in most of them the problems of collectivization, and of "primitive accumulation" (at the peasants' expense) to finance industrialization, are still major factors in party policy, perhaps taking priority -- as they used to do in the USSR -- over questions of agricultural production and efficiency. The satellite countries are not all in the same position in these respects. Thus Czechoslovakia, already highly industrialized, is offering favorable prices to its collectivized peasants and apparently securing some cooperation from them. By contrast, Poland and Hungary have achieved some agricultural recovery by giving more freedom to private peasants, and they must face an acute crisis if, and when, the drive for collectivization is resumed, as in Hungary.

However, in discussing the possible increases in yields from existing land, it would be wrong to overstress ideology and organization. In the last analysis, the problem is one of work, of inputs. A cow of a given breed, which is properly fed and looked after, does not give less milk merely by reason of being owned by a collective farm. Poor soils in north Germany provide much higher crops than similar soils in northwestern USSR largely because of much greater application of fertilizer, and fertilizer is, in itself, a politically neutral inanimate object. The low productivity of Russian farm land and animals is a fact.

But, precisely because the potentialities were poorly utilized -- mainly owing to concentration on industrial growth -- the unexhausted possibilities of major improvements are there. In particular, even Khrushchev himself, the archapostle of extensive farming in marginal steppelands, has noted the possibility of greatly increasing production on the podsol soils of the northwest, where droughts are unknown and where yields are at present extremely low. 7/ There is widespread dissatisfaction at the low output of mineral fertilizer, and one of the objects of the drive to expand the chemical industry is to increase it. The present situation is illustrated in Table 4.

This table shows the extent to which the available supplies have been

Table 4

Fertilizer Use, USSR and West Germany, 1956
(Soviet [gross] units of mineral fertilizer per hectare of ploughland)

USSR: Nonblack-earth center	56
USSR: Central Asian republics	371
German Federal Republic	803

Source: Borkov, Ekonomika Selskovo Khozaistva, No. 5/1958, p. 43. The "nonblack-earth center" covers the central area of European Russia, north of the black-earth belt.

used for special crops -- notably cotton in Central Asia -- so that little is left for other areas or for other crops. It is therefore important to note that the seven-year plan envisages increasing mineral fertilizer deliveries from 10.3 to 31 million tons.

The potentialities for a durable increase in yields are less promising on the better quality lands of the south and east. There the soil is more fertile, but the danger of drought remains great. It is probably not rational to use fertilizer there on a large scale, and it is noteworthy that little is used on similar types of land in Canada. In the very long term, afforestation and irrigation can doubtless modify the situation, but the failure of Stalin's "plan to transform nature" -- most of the forest belts did not in fact grow -- is a warning against expecting rapid results.

On balance, Soviet land resources should make possible a quite significant improvement in Soviet farm production and therefore in nutritional standards. The ambitious targets set for 1965, however, will prove to be beyond the realms of practical possibility, and striving to achieve them may cause serious distortions in farm policy, of which the renewed central pressure to expand corn sowings in unsuitable areas appears to be one. It may also affect adversely the industrialized satellites, which are net importers of grain and rely greatly on the USSR for their supplies. After the good harvest year 1956, the Soviet Union was able to export 7.5 million tons of grain. A higher figure may be reached after the even better harvest of 1958. But, if the meat program is to make progress, Soviet animals will eat up much of the grain surplus. Indeed, the new farm prices show a very great rise in meat prices in relation to all others and this undoubtedly reflects the intention to encourage feeding of grain to livestock. 8/ If planned internal grain utilization is based on harvests of 180 million tons, then the inevitable shortfall will leave the satellites heavily dependent on grain imports from outside the bloc.

INVESTMENT AND GROWTH

So far, we have been concerned with physical availabilities, and with natural resources in relation to the very ambitious growth targets of the

15

bloc. However, it is also necessary to consider the possibility of developing these resources, bearing in mind the relative scarcity of the means required for such development. The special problem of manpower will be considered in a separate section, below. Here it is intended to discuss the extent of the investment effort which will be required, and in particular whether the high "growth-effectiveness" of investment in the Soviet world is a temporary or durable phenomenon.

This last point is of high importance. It has been argued 9/ that the share of national income devoted to fixed investment in the USSR has not greatly exceeded that of the United States. Against this view, it can be objected that the Soviet price pattern artificially cheapens investment goods as against consumers' goods, even when corrected into "adjusted factor cost," because of the systematic preference accorded to heavy industry in the allocation of modern equipment and efficient managers. This interpretation receives strong support from the trend of relative prices within the USSR. Thus the percentage devoted to investment would be higher in the USSR if the goods concerned were valued in dollars rather than current rubles, or in constant rubles of an earlier date.

Nonetheless, despite the inevitable imprecision and contradictoriness of the data, it remains a reasonable conclusion that growth in the USSR has exceeded that of the United States by more than can be explained by a superior percentage of GNP devoted to investment. There must, therefore, be circumstances other than the sheer volume of investment which explain the superior growth rate. Why has a given unit of investment generated more growth in the USSR, and will it do so in the future?

One of the "advantages" of the Soviet world is the relative "youth" of its fixed capital. A high proportion of Soviet factories was built comparatively recently. As a result, a smaller proportion of gross investment is used for replacement than is the case in older industrial countries. The Soviet depreciation allowances tend to be too low, but, in any case, the ratio of net to gross investment must be higher in countries which have come relatively recently into the stage of industrialization. This is, by definition, an advantage which cannot last. Thus in the Soviet Union much of the equipment erected in the first two five-year plans is by now wearing out, or is obsolete. The drive for all out economic growth often led to neglect of proper maintenance, and the very idea of obsolescence was disregarded until 1955 by Soviet planners and economists alike. The situation is now changing, and this will gradually eliminate one of the factors which tended to make Soviet investment more "effective" in terms of generating higher output -- although China will still benefit from it.

Of course, neglect of maintenance or proper replacement is not in itself a healthy phenomenon, and is hardly beneficial for growth. Yet in the short run it can help to jack up the figures, although at the cost of trouble for the future. For example, the production achievements of the fifties were accompanied by a chronic underfulfillment of investment plans (see Table 5). Thus plans had to be fulfilled by overworking existing capacity -- though the process was doubtless assisted by the existence of so-called "hidden reserves" -- that is, unreported productive potential, which provides managers with a "safety margin." 10/ It is true that if the capital stock grows at a constant rate, the ratio of gross to net investment should not be affected merely by the passage of time. But any slowdown in the rate

Table 5

Fulfillment of Soviet Plans, 1953-56
(Percent)

	1953	1954	1955	1956
Investment volume	89.9	93.5	94.7	97.4
Completions of prod. capacity	82.8	88.3	88.3	83.1

Source: Sokolov, Voprosy Ekonomiki, No.11/1958, p. 40.

of additions to basic capital is more than proportionately reflected in the relative slowdown of net investment.

There was another consequence of the policy of all out expansion. Up and down the Soviet hierarchy, men were judged by their ability to overfulfill current plans, and longer-term considerations were often sacrificed in consequence. For example, iron ore or coal mines were "creamed," the best and most easily accessible mineral being taken as quickly as possible. This was and is in part due to lack of long-term responsibility on the part of those in charge of operations; by the time the consequences of their actions become visible, they will have been moved elsewhere -- meanwhile, they will have received bonuses and perhaps the Red Banner for having achieved results in the present plan period.

This same mental approach is often to be seen in Soviet agriculture. The virgin lands campaign was launched with little consideration of the long-term problem of soil conservation. Other agricultural campaigns - notably corn -- have tended repeatedly to disorganize crop rotations in the interests of immediate results, so much so that one character in a Soviet short story sadly remarked: "Perhaps I will live long enough to see the day when just one crop rotation scheme will be completed." 11/ Similarly, angry articles by forestry conservation experts refer to the ruthless cutting of trees in the most accessible areas.

All this has direct relevance to future growth, and helps to explain the high tempos of the past. Clearly, there will be a tendency toward diminishing returns to a given amount of investment effort under the circumstances, other things being equal. One of the things which may not be equal is, of course, the progress of technique, which must tend partly to offset this trend. Thus the great effort to expand synthetics is due, among other reasons, to a realization that major savings are possible in this way. The extent to which technical progress will alter the picture is largely a matter of opinion and conjecture. On the whole, it seems unlikely to alter decisively the trend toward diminishing returns, yet it would be dangerous to neglect the possibility of unexpectedly large returns to the big efforts made in fundamental research.

Both the USSR and China require major investment in transportation. It is a remarkable fact, for instance, that the USSR's network of paved roads is still smaller than that of Great Britain. There is still little long-distance road traffic. Most Russian villages are cut off in spring and autumn, owing to mud-bound roads. This not only impedes production but tends to depress living standards. Poor transportation is one of the reasons for the deplorable lack of shopping and other amenities in rural areas.

A very heavy load is thrown on the railroads. In the USSR they still carry over four fifths of all traffic. A great deal has been done to increase the efficiency of the railroads, and there is a truly remarkable intensity of utilization of tracks and rolling stock. The Soviet railroads now carry nearly four times as much goods per track mile as the American, and the disparity is greater still in passenger traffic. Since 1913, traffic has increased in the USSR more than ninefold, but track mileage has only doubled.

The Soviet policy has been, here as elsewhere, to achieve quick results. As far as possible, investment in new lines, or new roads, has been kept to a minimum. But now, as Soviet economists insist, the stage of saturation has been reached. The situation calls for "very substantial capital investments." 12/ It is pointed out by them that the present rate of new track construction is only a fraction of what it was in 1913.

All the above relates primarily to the "old" territories, where the growing traffic is too much for available facilities. But we must also take into account the developments which are now being planned in remote areas, in both Siberia and China, where at the moment there are no roads or railways at all. A totally new network will be required. Investments in transportation are part of the cost of industrial and agricultural expansion. These costs have been kept at a minimum and must now increase. Here is another urgent claim which must be met out of the resources available for investment, or of the needs of underdeveloped countries outside the bloc.

Finally, the increasing demands of the citizens on investment resources are of very real importance in the present context. The point has already been made earlier, and it suffices here to emphasize the fact that the apparently superior "growth-effectiveness" of Soviet investment has been in part due to neglect of unproductive investments, especially of housing. The efforts being made to repair past neglect must mean the diversion of labor and materials to the erection of dwellings, the manufacture of drainpipes, window frames, glass, roofing, baths, sinks, and the rest. 13/ The need to do more for the ordinary citizen is recognized also in the European satellites, in varying degrees. Thus plans have been revised in this direction in Poland and Hungary.

Some Western critics consider that greater attention to the consumer needs should show itself in a change in ratio of investment to consumption, or to a higher relative output of consumers' goods. They point to the output plans now adopted, and to the makeup of the investment plans for 1959-65 (given in Table 6), and they sometimes assert that the shift in priorities is not real. There are several answers to these objections, though it is clear enough that the highest priority for heavy industry remains the feature of Soviet planning.

First, many of the most urgent needs of the citizens require investment in houses, drains, retail stores, and the like. The effect of such investments on industrial output is to stimulate still further the output of such producers' goods as building materials and pipes. The change is in the use to which they are put. The end result does not take the form of consumers' goods. Low rents cause an undervaluation of housing services, while the

18

advantages of shorter queues in shops or a piped water supply fail to show in national income accounts.

Second, the bulk of the period 1952-58, with which the investment plan of 1959-65 is statistically compared, relates to the post-Stalin years, when many of the tendencies we have been discussing were already operating.

Third, in making comparisons with earlier periods, the biggest relative change does not appear in the state's investment accounts; a very large increase has occurred in investments in agriculture financed by collective farms, and in housing financed by individuals (out of savings or with the help of bank credits). While not a financial burden to the state, this diverts into farming and private building many commodities ("producers' goods") made by state industry, and contributes to a change in the extent to which industry is orientated primarily to the further growth of industry.

All the factors mentioned in the preceding pages have the effect of diminishing the growth generated by each unit of investment, as compared with the results of past years. Another way of saying the same thing is this: The economy has been stretched to the greatest possible extent in order to maximize industrial growth; this has led to a whole number of disproportions, which are becoming intolerable (economically, technically, socially). There is an urgent need to right imbalances, to correct lopsided development. But this inevitably leads to some slowdown in growth.

A CAPITAL SHORTAGE?

It has been argued in the preceding pages that there are grounds for expecting a severe strain on capital resources, if a high industrial growth rate is to be combined with other objectives now being pursued by the Soviet leadership. Some measure of the extent of the strain may be gauged from studying the investments envisaged in the seven-year plan. The only available basis of comparison, shown in Table 6, is the actual expenditure of the previous seven years -- in other words, the total for 1959-65 is compared with the total for 1952-58, unlike the various industrial and agricultural targets, which are given for the single year 1965, usually in comparison with 1958. 14/ The increase from 1958 to 1965 is smaller than appears from the table -- hardly more than 75 percent, the precise figure depending on the shape of the investment "curve" in the years in question.

The plan for 1956-60, now abandoned, envisaged investments in the national economy of a total value of 990 billion rubles, in what seems to be virtually the same prices, for the five years. This was to represent an increase of 67 percent over the volume of investment in the five years 1951-55. Clearly, the new seven-year plan sets a formidable task in the investment sector. For the many reasons emphasized above, strains are bound to emerge in the course of the attempt to carry out this task. These strains can be viewed as a form of capital shortage. Of course, this will not be a financial shortage; forced savings via the budget can be increased to the desired extent.

19

Table 6

Expenditures on Fixed Investment, USSR, 1952-58 and Planned 1959-65
(Billion rubles)

	1952-58 actual	1959-65 plan b/	Increase percent
Total, National economy a/	1,072	1,955	82.4
of which:			
Ferrous metallurgy d/	40.8	100	144
Chemical industry	19.9	102.5	415
Oil and gas	72.2	171.5	140
Coal	61.2	76.5	24
Electricity (incl. transmission)	75.1	127	69
Machinery	65.5	118	80
Timber, paper	25.3	59	136
Light and food industry	40	82.5	106
Building materials and building industry	61.5	111	82
Agriculture, state	n.a.	150	n.a.
(Agriculture, all) c/	(260)	(500)	(92)
Transport and communications	107.4	211.5	97
Housing and communal	214	378	77
Education, health, culture	46	"over 80"	75

a/ Excluding collective-farm, cooperative and individual investments.
b/ Mid-points of range.
c/ Includes collective farms, but not individuals.
d/ Including iron ore.
Source: Reconstructed from Pravda, Moscow, November 14, 1958 and January 28, 1959.

The strains will appear in the form of physical shortages. Thus the plan for building labor envisages a rise in productivity per head of as much as 60-65 percent in seven years, despite a cut in hours. If this is not achieved, then a holdup in building could cause further holdups in production of various commodities vital to the plan. It is true that the seven-year plan has been very carefully prepared, with the active participation of many prominent academicians in various sectional subcommittees. 15/ There is a logical coherence in the plan and in its various investment projects. 16/ But strains can still arise when they are all combined.

It can be argued that no one project is unattainable. New industrial areas can and will be developed, new roads and railways built, the chemical industry greatly expanded, the housing program speeded up, and so on. But the question remains whether all these aims can be effectively pursued within a relatively short historical period, whether the achievements of the past decade have not accustomed Soviet planners to underestimate the requirements of their program. We may expect conflicts of priorities, when the overfull commitment of resources compels the authorities to cut something, and unexpected scarcities may frequently arise, although we cannot at this stage tell where such strains will show themselves.

The existence of these strains expresses itself in the much greater consciousness of the problem of scarcity and in the attention devoted to efficiency in the use of resources, of which more will be said. This has affected the investment program itself, and Khrushchev has sought to economize investment resources by abandoning part of his hydroelectric schemes in favor of less capital-intensive variants. It must also affect the whole attitude of the bloc to foreign trade, simultaneously limiting the room for "political" maneuver and encouraging economically rational deals. This too will have to be dealt with later.

MANPOWER

In any consideration of resources for growth and economic competition, it is evident that the availability and quality of labor must be given a key place. Especially relevant in our present context are not only the aggregate size and growth of the population, but also the present utilization of manpower. Much of the growth-potential of comparatively underdeveloped countries arises from the possibility of transferring underemployed and/or inefficiently used peasant labor into industrial employment. Table 7 contains relevant basic data.

It is clear that Soviet growth has not been due to an abnormally rapid rise in the total population. On the contrary, owing to the vast losses in the war, numbers have increased little since 1940. It must also be stressed that war losses in births are now adversely affecting the intake of new labor in the USSR, and will continue to do so for several years yet. This "delayed" effect of the war cannot be seen in the labor statistics, but the extreme importance of this matter can be illustrated by citing figures for the school population, as shown in Table 8.

Those who were 7 to 10 years old in 1953-54 have made their way up through the educational system, and are now emerging into working age. Soviet planning must, therefore, be operating in the knowledge that new labor is much less abundant than had been customary in the past. This probably helps to explain, among other things, the drastic educational reform announced in September 1958 (of which more below). After about 1963, however, the rapid natural increase in Russia's population will have a positive effect on growth capabilities, especially in comparison with the countries of Western Europe, though the United States is almost level with the USSR in this respect.

Turning now to manpower utilization, it is clear that Soviet economic growth has to a large extent depended on transfers from village to town. The available statistics are somewhat misleading, since there are no precise figures of working farmers, military personnel or prisoners, but some statistics, for what they are worth, are presented in Table 9.

It is impossible to express with any exactitude the decline in the number of peasants during the period. The rural population as a whole fell, according to the official data, from 131 million in 1940 to 113 million in 1956, 17/ but this almost certainly understates the shift: There are many nonfarming

Table 7

Population Data, Sino-Soviet Bloc and Selected Western Nations

	Total Population (millions)		Percent in Agri- culture	Birth Rate (per thousand)	Death Rate
	1940	1956	1956	1956	1956
USSR	{191.7 a/ 〈195 a/	200.2	43 c/	25.0	7.7 g/
China (Mainland)	–	621.2	(80)	37 d/	17 d/
Czechoslovakia	14.7	13.2	33	19.8	9.6
East Germany	–	17.7	20.5	15.8	11.9
Hungary	9.3	9.8	44	19.6	10.6
Poland	34.6 b/	27.8	53	27.9	9.0
Rumania	15.9	17.6	69	24.2	9.9
United States	132.1	168.2	9.5	24.9	9.4
United Kingdom	48.3	51.2	5.2	16.1	11.7
West Germany	–	50.5	23.1 e/	16.5	11.2
France	39.8	43.6	28.9	18.5	12.5
Japan	71.4	90.0	41.1 f/	18.5	8.0

a/ Official estimate is 191.7. However, this is an understatement; see Nove and Newth, Bulletin of Oxford University Institute of Statistics, February 1957.
b/ Prewar territory.
c/ Percent of a total which excludes military personnel.
d/ 1953 (Peking People's Daily, November 1, 1954).
e/ 1950.
f/ 1955.
g/ Seems suspiciously low.
Figures in parentheses are rough approximations.
Source: Official statistics, and U.N. Economic Commission for Europe, Economic Survey of Europe 1957.

Table 8

Millions of Soviet Children in Classes I-IV
(Age groups, approx. 7-10)

1940/41	21.4
1948/49	23.7
1953/54	12.1

Source: Kulturnoe Stroitelstvo SSSR 1956, p. 122.

occupations followed in rural areas, and there was a high proportion of women and old men in the villages after the war. According to the same official source, of the total gainfully employed population (exclusive of military, prisoners and perhaps some others), 80 percent were in agriculture in 1928, 56 percent in 1937, and 43 percent in 1956.

Table 9

State Nonfarm Labor Force, USSR
(Millions)

	1937	1950	1956
Total	24.4	35.8	44.7
of which: Industry a/	10.1	14.1	18.6
Construction	1.6	2.6	3.4

a/ Extractive and manufacturing.
Source: Narodnoe Khozaistvo SSSR v 1956 godu.

It is true that this figure of 43 percent is far above that of any developed Western country. Correspondingly, the yet unrealized opportunities of economizing in agricultural manpower, and shifting it to industrial occupations, are much greater in the USSR than in, say, the United States. That such opportunities do exist in Russian villages can hardly be doubted by anyone who has seen them. This generalization applies with at least equal force to such satellites as Poland or Rumania. Yet, so far as the USSR is concerned, it would be quite wrong to expect this process to work itself out smoothly. On the contrary, the agricultural campaigns since Stalin's death have led to a net increase in the agricultural labor force. Thus in 1956, there were 2.6 million more collective farmers of working age than in 1953. 18/ There was also a major transfer of technically competent persons into agriculture, 19/ as well as a substantial rise in numbers employed in industries serving farm needs, such as in the construction of elevators and storehouses, handling fuel destined for farm use, making farm machinery, and so on.

No doubt large savings of labor in agriculture are possible, and the seven-year plan does envisage some reduction in the farm labor force. But a change in long-established habits of labor utilization cannot be achieved quickly, and in the short run the effort to expand agricultural production has required more people. Further progress depends on a major re-equipment of agriculture, and therefore on a balanced and expanded program of agricultural investment.

There are also a number of other major causes of strain in the labor market. Thus the ambitious investment plans call for more workers to build the new houses and factories, to settle the developing areas of Siberia. The regime is also publicly committed to reduce hours of labor from 46 to 42 a week by 1960, 20/ and has now declared itself for a 40-hour week by 1962 and a 35-hour week later in the decade.

Bearing in mind the delayed effects of low wartime births, it is clear that problems of the most effective utilization of the available labor force are among the most vital questions faced by Soviet administrators and economists. The reduction in the numbers of soldiers has done something to relieve the situation, but can hardly alter matters in any fundamental way. 21/ The USSR must now rely to a much greater extent on increases in labor productivity to maintain its growth tempos. This goes far to explain the preoccupation with efficiency in the use of resources which has been a feature of the post-Stalin period. The seven-year plan demands an increase

23

of 45-50 percent in industrial productivity per head. While this looks moderate in relation to past Soviet claims, it represents much more than this on a per hour basis. Strumilin, in his letter to the London Times (December 31, 1958), claimed that an 80 percent increase per hour would be involved. In other words, the increase in total output is wholly accounted for by the increase in hourly productivity.

Some critics see a contradiction between the view that there is a labor shortage in the USSR and the fact that labor is wastefully used in agriculture, that there is often difficulty in finding work for juveniles, and also that hours are being reduced. Yet these facts do not invalidate the argument. Obviously, by Western standards, labor is often wastefully used; that is why Soviet productivity per head is so much lower (especially in agriculture) than it is in the United States. It is also true that juveniles, attending schools in western cities in which industrial expansion is kept in check, find little opportunity in those cities. This is a geographic question: The jobs tend to be in new areas, into which many young citizens of Moscow and Leningrad are understandably reluctant to go. There are also the usual problems of frictional unemployment and temporary maladjustments, inevitable in any society.

The agricultural labor surplus often consists of peasant women with families, who cannot easily be transformed into building laborers or factory hands a thousand or more miles away. There is also a shortage of farm labor at peak periods, and new machines must be designed to achieve all-round economy. All these things take time. Meanwhile, the argument still holds that labor of the right qualifications is short in the places in which it is needed. The effect of the reduction in hours is thus to make the increase in hourly labor productivity equal to the planned increase in industrial output in the seven years, although the resumption of a rapid rate of intake of new labor after 1963, when postwar births reach working age, must be expected to improve the situation considerably.

Labor shortage may well prove a most important obstacle to rapid growth in the Soviet Union. At this point it may be apt to contrast this situation with that of China. If the bloc as a whole were a single political unit, with free immigration, one could hardly continue to speak of labor shortage. Yet, for reasons quite unconnected with Communist internationalism, there is little likelihood of any large-scale use of Chinese labor in the USSR or in the satellites, save possibly some ad hoc borrowing on a strictly temporary basis. China herself starts from a situation of relative labor abundance, and this has greatly influenced the communist leaders' ideas about Chinese economic development. 22/ After at first seeking to copy the Soviet pattern, China has been launched on a vast new program of rural industrialization, and aims at a rate of investment and development so rapid as to absorb all surplus labor, and indeed the tendency now is to compel the people to work with unexampled intensity.

In pursuing this policy, the Chinese leaders are being as intelligent as they are ruthless. Given the aim of achieving record-breaking growth rates, in a situation in which capital is scarce and the bulk of the people are in villages, it is certainly logical to adopt labor-intensive, capital-saving variants, using the labor where it is and avoiding the heavy expenses of urbanization. However, communist economic campaigns generally overshoot the mark, and the present policy of overstraining the people in order

24

to produce anything under any conditions and at any cost will no doubt achieve much waste, as well as big percentage increases in output. It is doubtful if the Chinese model will be found relevant for the USSR or European bloc countries, although the expansion of small-scale industrial activities in villages has for some time attracted the Soviet authorities. Indeed, in many areas the peasants used to derive much of their cash from handicrafts, and Stalin's deliberate policy killed most of these activities, although some such developments, in moderation, would make good sense.

QUALITY OF LABOR AND EDUCATION

Throughout the Soviet world, there is great faith in the advantages to be gained through education, which is expected to facilitate technical progress and greatly to improve the quality of the labor force. Communist ideology lays such great stress on education that the effort made in this direction sometimes outshoots practical requirements and even leads to social (and perhaps political) instability. Such extremes may perhaps be seen in the promise made at the 20th Party Congress in 1956, to extend full secondary education to all Soviet children by 1960, and it has been found necessary to take a major step backwards, involving the breaking of this promise, in the autumn of 1958. The average Soviet child is now to cease full-time education at 15 to 16, and part of the university course is to be part-time also.

While this is no place to discuss the complex motivation and possible consequences of this step backwards in Soviet education, it seems probable that labor shortage, and the anxiety to ensure the greater productive efficiency of the intake of young people, have played an important part in causing these decisions to be taken. The educational effort will remain impressive, by any standard, especially taking into account the exacting nature of the Soviet high school curriculum. 23/ Other bloc countries are also developing their education with vigor. For example, Poland has 125,000 full-time students, while Great Britain has only 85,000 despite its much larger population. The various schemes of lower-level technical training are, if anything, even more remarkable.

One factor, which may play an appreciable role, is the higher social standing in the USSR of education as such, and the greater keenness of youth to acquire knowledge and skills. This is partly due to traditional attitudes, partly to deliberate encouragement, partly to the material incentives offered, and finally, perhaps to the relative absence of counterattractions and of what might be called the commercialization of the moron. The impact on the underdeveloped world, where education is often the subject almost of reverence, can be serious on a propaganda level. It can affect underdeveloped countries more directly if students are invited in greater numbers to study in the USSR. And, finally, the increasing production of Soviet technicians will probably permit the dispatch of more of them to work in Asian and African countries.

The development of education in the Soviet bloc undoubtedly outpaces the West. Yet, if one is to keep a sense of proportion, it must not be forgotten that this more rapid tempo is directly related to past backwardness.

25

There are greater efforts needed to train a peasant lad to handle machinery than are called for in a developed urban community. Much of the knowledge acquired in Russian "technicums" is picked up on the job in America or England. Then, we in the West have a bigger reservoir of managerial and technical skills to draw upon.

The speed of Soviet industrialization was such that it outpaced the training programs, and so for many years the economy suffered from having to "make do" with inferior managers, technicians, and craftsmen. Soviet nonpriority sectors still suffer from this today. One has only to contemplate the organization of retail trading and catering establishments, or to observe the quality of paint work, plumbing, or carpentry. Gradually, the better-educated new generation will surely improve matters. There is less scope for such improvement in the West, simply because of our relatively higher general standards of efficiency.

Therefore, the rate of increase in labor productivity should remain higher in the USSR than in the West. How much higher will depend on a large number of other factors: the pace of technical progress, possible developments in automation, the ability of the system to adjust itself to the requirements of economically rational use of resources, and so on. It would be pointless to attempt at this stage a quantitative evaluation of all these "unknowns." It is sufficient to stress that the carrying out of Soviet plans imposes the necessity of ensuring the most effective utilization of the available labor force, and that much of the Soviet economic and social policy is at present directed toward seeking ways of doing this. This will be further discussed in the next chapter.

Chapter Three

INTERNAL ECONOMIC ORGANIZATION

INTRODUCTION

In the preceding section, we have been discussing resources and their utilization -- with the emphasis on the physical problems of expansion. The problems of organization and efficiency are equally vital. Few can doubt that, by concentrating resources on (say) steelworks and oil wells, the USSR and its allies can greatly increase the output of these and other commodities. However, the object of production is the satisfaction of wants, and impressive statistical results can be achieved which do not represent an analogous real gain. For example, the labor and materials which enter into the construction of a half-completed factory, which is then abandoned, appear in the national income accounts, but the resources are nonetheless wasted. A steelworks in the wrong place produces steel, and calls for the construction of railroad tracks, freight cars and other goods and services, but production can still be uneconomic and can lead to a loss which is nonetheless real for being concealed. The existence of such waste in the Soviet world (and not only in the Soviet world!) leads naturally to a consideration of the advantages and problems which arise from the special features of the Soviet economic system.

EFFICIENCY IN PLANNING AND PRODUCTION

Questions of efficiency and of the economic effectiveness in the utilization of resources have been figuring prominently in the Soviet press since Stalin's death. Nor is this fact simply due to the death of the dictator. In the early stages of "forced industrialization," Stalin directed maximum resources toward the top-priority aim of laying the foundations of industrial might -- that is, the development of heavy industry -- and also toward the strengthening of Soviet military potential. These aims remain high on the Soviet state of priorities, of course. However, as has been shown earlier, there are now other priorities which complicate planning and impose additional strains on available resources. Then the rapid increase in the size and complexity of the economy imposes new organizational strains. Finally, as has already been demonstrated, the available resources have to be stretched to the uttermost to cover the many requirements imposed by the program of competitive growth.

For all these reasons, there has been a much greater consciousness of the problem of efficiency. Because labor is becoming short (due partly to the temporary effects of the low wartime births), there is particular anxiety to avoid waste of labor. This has shown itself in a number of ways: in the

27

revival of economic theory from its deep sleep, in the reduction of the numbers in the armed forces, in a re-examination (and therefore partial abandonment) of forced labor as a means of economic development. There has also been review of the forms and principles of economic organization. This is by no means confined to the USSR. Thus a reform of planning of considerable importance was introduced in Czechoslovakia in April 1958, and there has been a great deal of fundamental discussion in Poland and to some extent also in Hungary and even East Germany. 1/

The defects of the Soviet economic structure, which were faithfully copied by (or imposed upon) the satellite states, may be summarized as follows:

1. Overcentralization. This was directly connected with the concentration of resources on priority tasks, but led to serious inefficiencies due to bureaucratic delays and discouragement of local initiative.

2. Lack of Objective Criteria for economic decision at local or enterprise levels. No theoretical or practical guide to action was developed, other than that of fulfilling the plan set from above. However, since plans could never cover all details or eventualities, the men on the spot had some freedom of action, and naturally tended to use it so as to fit their performance into the plan "indicators." In this way the managers could both maximize their own bonuses and win the approval of their superiors. Therefore, if the plan were expressed in tons, there was a tendency to make heavy articles, if in length, long and narrow articles, if in numbers, small articles; if in money, relatively expensive articles. Also, insofar as the management was involved in drafting the plan, there was direct inducement to conceal production possibilities so as to have an "easy" plan. All these things led the central authorities to intervene in great detail, to ensure that the right things were produced, and this contributed to bureaucratic overcentralization.

3. Illogicalities of the Price System. To this day, no agreed criterion for price-fixing has been devised by Soviet economists and planners. Prices have been arbitrarily determined, generally at the center. But if prices did not conform to any logical pattern, this inevitably deprived both the enterprises and the planners of an essential basis of judgment. There was no link, through prices and profitability, between the demand pattern and the process of production, since the prices were unresponsive to demand. Prices did not reflect relative scarcities of materials, and this rendered inevitable strict central allocation of most materials. Arbitrary pricing at all stages deprived the authorities of criteria for choice between investment alternatives, and led to expensive errors. Investment decisions were also confused by a tendency to vary freight charges without regard to cost, 2/ and by the refusal to give explicit recognition to the rate of interest as a guide to the allocation of scarce central resources.

4. Failures of the Material Supply Organization. This was due partly to the existence of clumsy central allocation schemes, but most of all to the imposition of such rapid growth tempos that there was chronic overcommitment of resources. Uncertainties in supply led to hoarding at enterprise level.

5. Lack of Reward for Risk-taking, and therefore a discouragement of

new ideas unless and until the center had approved them. The very idea that risk should be rewarded has received no recognition.

6. The Influence of the Calendar caused an unhealthy concentration on fulfilling the current plan, to the detriment of longer-term considerations. In the short run it leads to the disease known as shturmovshchina, or the mad rush to fulfill the monthly plan schedules which usually causes disorganization in the weeks following. In the long run it causes neglect of resource conservation in the interest of immediate results.

Some critics may ask how, if such defects as those could exist, it was possible to achieve such rapid growth rates. Such a question shows a misunderstanding: It is because of centralized planning for maximum growth that these defects have arisen -- they are part of the cost. At a given stage of economic and social development, they are tolerated. Perhaps for the next decade or so they will be tolerated in China. For reasons already outlined, they have become intolerable in the USSR. They were never justified in more advanced countries, such as Czechoslovakia and Hungary; they were imposed there as part of the compulsory copying of the Soviet pattern.

A new, more flexible, more efficient system must be found, if the bloc is rapidly to raise its economy from present levels to compete with developed western countries, and if it is to impress the underdeveloped world with the superiority of its system. The bloc can, and does, point to certain advantages of planning: the avoidance of recessions, the coordination of investment decisions, the minimization of waste of resources on advertising and imports of expensive cars and soft drinks; of these more will be said in due course. It would gain much, not only in operational efficiency but also in its ability to influence people, if some at least of the defects could be eliminated.

Earnest efforts are being made to find ways and means of doing this. The various problems are closely interlinked: Thus, the only substitute for the price mechanism as a guide to action is administrative orders, and to base operations on such orders is to invite the inefficiencies of centralized bureaucracy with all that it implies. Therefore discussions in the Soviet world are, reasonably enough, concerned both with price policy and with decentralization.

Decentralization has, in fact, been tackled first. There are, in principle, three possible approaches: to devolve authority to regions, to economic sectors (ministries), or to enterprises.

After Stalin's death, there was some limited increase in the powers of republics and enterprises, but the greatest emphasis was on strengthening the powers of economic ministries. The ministries, however, tended to look after the needs of "their" enterprises, to the detriment of desirable regional coordination. Separate supply and disposal systems caused duplication, and each ministry tended to make itself independent of outside supplies as far as possible, by setting up workshops of its own. There were numerous examples of waste. The disadvantages of this so-called "departmentalism," together with political considerations which fall outside the scope of this paper, led to a major reform in May 1957. Almost all economic ministries were abolished, their powers being largely transferred to the republics and regions. Gosplan and the Council of Ministers were to exercise powers of coordination.

This solution would seem to substitute "regionalism" for "departmentalism," without solving the essential problem. While local coordination may be better managed, interregional relations are likely to be disrupted by autarkic tendencies. The existence of these tendencies is recognized, and the Soviet authorities have threatened the officials concerned with punishment for failure to observe interregional supply obligations. However, threats of punishment are not a sound basis for ensuring efficient operation of a delicate process. The problem remains: to devise economic criteria, by which regional (or any other) economic authorities can be guided and judged. Without such criteria, all decentralization schemes suffer from a crucial defect: Whereas at the center it is at least theoretically possible to calculate physical need on a national scale, a regional planning authority has no means of determining what is needed outside its own boundaries, and so, with the best will in the world, it is unable to discover how to act in an economically rational manner. Naturally it tends to give priority to its own needs. 3/ Not surprisingly, the real extent of decentralization has been modest.

Regionalization in the USSR is to some extent explicable by the sheer size of the country, and other methods are being tried elsewhere. 4/ Thus in Czechoslovakia a functional rather than a regional solution is being tried, with much greater authority given to enterprises and trusts, and much more freedom of contract than exists in the Soviet system. 5/

However, neither the Soviet nor the Czech variant grapple with the vital problem of price formation. The logical basis of the necessary decentralization is leaving the enterprises free (or at least freer) to respond to stimuli of price and profit. The question of who decides the price is of the greatest social-political significance, for, if prices were to fluctuate in accordance with the supply and demand situation, this would mean that the producers would tend to obey the dictates of the market rather than those of the planning authorities. Such a line of thought runs counter to fundamental Marxist notions; it is repeatedly asserted by Soviet theoreticians that the plan, the decisions of "Society," must be primary, that "the law of value" (that is, the spontaneous economic forces) does not and should not have a "regulatory" function in a socialist society.

Free price fluctuation, a free market, are among the heinous "sins of revisionism" of which the Yugoslav leadership is held to be guilty. The government, the planning authorities, the party officials, seem instinctively to feel that their position as controllers depends on setting severe limits to the operation of economic forces. 6/ It is also remarkably difficult to devise a theoretical basis for price formation within the thought pattern of Marxist orthodoxy. Yet the price problem lies at the heart of the present difficulties. 7/ These difficulties greatly affect foreign trade also. The absence of a rational price system renders extremely difficult the necessary calculation of comparative advantage. A Czech economist would be hard put to it to decide whether, at a given world price, the export of a given article is, on balance, profitable.

It has been argued that these weaknesses are not serious, because, in the USSR, the use of resources and investment policy was not significantly influenced by the admittedly irrational prices. In one sense this is true. Clearly, the planners have not been guided by relative profitabilities in making their decisions, which were generally consequential upon a rudimentary form of input-output analysis -- to achieve A we need B, therefore manufacture more of B and build a new factory if capacity is insufficient. Prices play no part in such a calculation. However, wrong decisions at the center can result from the habit of disregarding the logic of prices and freights. Decisions on the utilization of resources, on the choice between investment alternatives, are by no means self-evident, and decisions which neglect prices and costs can be wrong, not by some abstract academic standard, but because they add unnecessarily to the real cost of attaining the desired result.

In a society in which this unnecessary cost can be made to fall on the consumer or on agriculture, this may not seem to matter, but the cost is there just the same. The economy is poorer than it need be. Resources are locked up in capital projects which are wrongly located or cannot be completed for lack of materials. The need for price rationality becomes much more urgent when some degree of (de jure or de facto) decentralization becomes a physical necessity, when it is found that the centralized "command economy" is unable to cope with the increasingly complex interrelationships of production, and because the freeing of initiative comes to be seen as indispensable for the achievement of high growth rates.

Lange wrote recently: "Methods which are necessary and useful in a period of social revolution and intensive industrialization become an obstacle to further economic progress if they are perpetuated beyond their economic justification .... They are rigid, they lead therefore to waste of resources." 8/ In the USSR itself, and in the party's own journal, economists argue for more "automatism" in economic life and for the sheer necessity of ending allocation of materials by administrative bodies. 9/ Soviet economists show increasing interest in econometrics, welcome Professor Leontief to Moscow, and study the applicability of Western economic techniques to their planning, because they are conscious of the inadequacy of the methods they have hitherto used to cope with the problems before them. 10/ It is not Western theoreticians, obsessed by Western notions of rationality, but economists of the Soviet world, who put these arguments.

On the other hand, it would be quite wrong to come to exaggerated conclusions about the relative inefficiency of the Soviet system as a whole. The "Stalinist" centralized-priority state was designed for a rapid industrialization program. Neither Lange, as the above quotation shows, nor the author of this paper, are arguing that it failed to do the job it set out to do. The cost, in terms of efficiency and human welfare, was heavy, but all out concentration on heavy industry is hardly possible if costs of this kind were carefully counted. However, now that a modern society with a well-developed heavy industry has been so largely built, the old methods, and the inefficiencies associated with them, must be changed. There is a search for forms suitable for what Lange, in the same article, has called a more mature Socialist society.

Meanwhile the system still works, still generates a high growth rate, is in no danger of collapse. Nor should we forget the many imperfections of the Western economy: underemployment of resources, monopolistic distortions, irrational "support" prices in agriculture, economically indefensible trade barriers, and much else besides. It is not a good thing to pander to the complacency of those who compare the often muddled reality of the USSR with the theoretical perfection of a model of the Western economy. Models and reality are two different things, in East and West alike.

In an important sense, existing political and ideological considerations have been inconsistent with the efficient operation of the economy. Because the political leadership gives very high priority to the economic competition with the West, it is likely to amend its ideas, and indeed we can witness the process going on before our eyes. Major changes in the price structure are obviously pending. There should be greater emphasis on interenterprise contracts as a basis of economic activity. There will be a greater stress on regularity as against arbitrariness. This could well have profound social effects, by strengthening the managerial strata and establishing legality on firmer foundations. It could also lead to conflict among the various interests involved: It is not a coincidence that the fall of Malenkov and Molotov in 1957 occured in the context of an argument about industrial decentralization. While the need for reform is widely understood, the leadership will seek to avoid changes which might threaten its power position, and there are signs of an anxious search for some middle way, which will ensure the primacy of political decisions over the general direction of the economy, while shedding the defects hitherto associated with central planning. It may be doubted whether such a halfway house exists. 11/ Certain improvements in the existing system may well be achieved, but a good deal of demonstrable and potentially avoidable inefficiency seems inseparable from the nature of the system.

THE SPECIAL PROBLEM OF AGRICULTURE

The problems of economic organization have a special significance in the field of agriculture for a number of historic and social reasons which are common to all the countries of the bloc.

The first difficulty peculiar to agriculture is the social-political problem presented by the peasantry. In varying degrees, by differing methods, each of the countries of the bloc has sought to expropriate peasant private property, to convert individual peasants into collective farmers -- though the process has had to be reversed (probably temporarily) in Hungary and Poland. The peasant's interest is seen to be inconsistent with the socialist transformation of society, and indeed this is largely so. But one consequence of this whole approach has been the subordination of economic organization to the quite "noneconomic" task of limiting peasant individualism. Efficient farmers were suppressed because individual farming was regarded as bad in itself.

Another historically explicable feature is the use of the collective farm system to exploit the rural population, to accumulate at their expense the resources needed for industrialization. This exploitation took the form of compulsory deliveries at nominal prices, and thus from the first involved the use of the price system as a form of barely disguised taxation, thereby

32

rendering it virtually useless as an economic measuring rod. Low prices meant basing state requirements, and collective production, on coercion, and farming responds particularly badly to bureaucratic orders.

One of the essential features of agricultural economics everywhere is land rent. In Soviet countries, explicit land rent payments were abolished with a flourish of trumpets. However, it is not easy to dispose of economic laws. The effect of the elimination of rent, allied to a policy of paying bonus prices for sales in excess of a fixed quota, was to penalize the less favorably situated farms, while giving an unreasonable advantage to those already favored by geography. Some attempts to vary delivery quotas, as a form of disguised differential rent, did little to correct the situation. There thus grew up big agricultural depressed areas, while a few farms prospered.

Still another dogma played a negative role: that of the cult of large farms. While in the steppelands the big farm has advantages, the dairy farming country with small fields -- typical of Russia's west and northwest, and of the Baltic states -- can be farmed with advantage by small units, on the Danish pattern. But no: Farms had to be large. There has been practically no study of optimum size, as if Marx had answered this question once for all.

These collective farms, often extremely poor, with delivery obligations to the state at inequitable prices, were and are nominally "co-operatives," with an elected management. Yet, clearly it was necessary for the state to ensure that these "false co-operatives" did not break up, and that they fulfilled their obligations. This led to several features peculiar to agriculture. One was the creation of the Machine Tractor Stations (MTS), which, controlling the machinery used by the collective farms, exercised a measure of supervision over them. Another was the close control which was exercised by local party officials over the farms; in no other branch of the economy was there so much party interference in everyday economic operations. Finally, to ensure that the farms produced what was wanted, despite the lack of material incentives, the central planners found it necessary to prescribe in great detail what each farm should do. The "elections" were in effect replaced by party appointment of farm officials.

These practices led to a number of weaknesses. First, the division between the farms and their machinery led to waste, inefficiency and conflicts. Second, constant interference from above subverted local initiative. The nature of agricultural production requires the taking of local circumstances into account, and failure to do so has been very costly. The tendency of the central authorities to embark on vast "campaigns," which have been imposed on farms from above, led to many an act which was economically and agronomically stupid.

Finally, the effect of the economic-organizational pattern imposed on agriculture has been to deprive the management of any means of relating costs to output. Imperfect though calculations have been in industry, they could serve as some guide to action; they have been almost nonexistent on the farms, for the following main reasons:

1. Multiple prices for each product, without any logical interrelationship, deprived money measurement of significance.

2. It is virtually impossible to find a way of measuring labor cost, owing to the nature of cash and kind distributions on collective farms.

3. The costs of inputs were just as illogical and confusing. Thus the economic value of this or that piece of farm machinery remained totally unknown.

The period 1953-58 has seen determined efforts in the USSR to correct organizational shortcomings in agriculture. It was – no doubt correctly – seen that no organizational changes can be a substitute for the provision of incentives, and so a drastic upward revision of prices formed an integral part of the reforms. This was followed, in 1958, by the abolition of the multiple-price system, so that collective farms sell to the state at one price. 12/ A series of changes have strengthened the authority of the farm management over the peasants, and their functions in deciding what the plan should be. The MTS are at present being abolished and their machinery is (at last) turned over to the collective farms. 13/ For example, Poland abolished her equivalent of MTS in 1956, and Czechoslovakia and Bulgaria followed the Soviet example.

The status of peasants vis-à-vis the collective, and of the collective in relation to state enterprises and the planning organs, is in process of probably far-reaching change at the moment of writing. The reforms so far implemented have undoubtedly contributed to the improved output figures achieved in recent years. However, many difficulties remain. While genuinely seeking efficiency, Soviet and party officials continue to subject the farm management to arbitrary interference, demanding the carrying out of "campaigns" (notably the corn campaign), or insisting on the adoption of "fashionable" methods such as square-cluster sowing or two-stage harvesting, regardless of local circumstances. The price system is much more logical than it was, but there is in the Soviet system a built-in reluctance to rely on economic inducements rather than on administrative orders.

Under Soviet conditions it is hard indeed to reproduce the highly-mechanized, highly-productive North American farm, when the system is wedded to size and complexity, with hordes of administrators, brigade leaders, accountants, piece rate calculators, agronomists, assistant agronomists, storekeepers, and watchmen. But no doubt an improvement over existing standards is possible, indeed highly probable. In any event, the substantial advances in productivity recorded recently in the USSR are unlikely to be typical of the bloc as a whole. In Poland and Hungary, progress has been conditional upon temporarily abandoning the battle of collectivization. If the process is ever to be resumed, there will be more trouble. In the USSR itself signs are multiplying of an offensive against the remnants of the private sector, and of efforts to move peasants into large "urban" villages, which will cause serious resentments if pressed too far.

China's efforts to industrialize are causing her to press more severely on the newly collectivised peasants. At the present time, China's villages are undergoing a fundamental transformation. It is far too soon to express a view about the efficacy of the rural communes, or about how the Chinese peasant will react to the drastic treatment which he is receiving. Past experience teaches that social revolution and economic rationality go ill together, and consequently one must expect much avoidable inefficiency. However, if labor is present in abundance, and/or if it is readily mobilizable and will work harder when told to do so -- which Russian peasants seldom did -- this would not constitute a bar to progress.

TECHNICAL AND SCIENTIFIC PROGRESS

It is obvious that the development and utilization of technical and scientific ideas is highly relevant to competitive capabilities. It is also clear that the nature of economic organization can encourage or discourage innovation, and can facilitate or confuse rational decisions about the desirability of this or that new technique. It is therefore necessary briefly to consider the Soviet system in relation to such questions as these.

The history of Soviet technical development so far has been very largely one of borrowing and adapting ready-made techniques and designs from advanced Western countries. Thus Gardner Clark noted this feature in the Soviet steel industry, and a Soviet writer 14/ has pointed out that most Soviet automobiles are exact copies of American ones. Mass-production methods are commonly copied from American models. The ability to utilize the experience of other nations on a mass scale, under conditions which ensure working to full capacity, allied to the absence of trade secrecy, has greatly facilitated Soviet economic progress. The publicity given to impressive Soviet achievements in the field of Sputniks, intercontinental missiles, and jet aircraft should not blind us to the fact that, outside of a very few fields, original applications of scientific knowledge to industrial processes in the USSR have been rare.

By now, many key sectors of Soviet industry have reached levels of technical efficiency which compare well with advanced Western countries. This is true, for instance, in steel, electric generation, and many branches of the machinery industry. There may now be diminishing returns to the borrowing of ideas from abroad, a greater necessity to rely on the application of Soviet discoveries. This statement, however, needs some qualification, because the industrial development of the USSR has been extremely uneven. Some sectors have hardly been touched by modernization -- for example, in textiles, clothing, and furniture, there is ample scope for fruitful copying of Western experience. Even in the priority industries, the full mechanization of basic processes is often accompanied by primitive hand operations in such processes as loading and unloading, materials handling, and fueling, while the clerical and accounting branches are notoriously ineffective.

So far, there has been a notable contrast between the quality of Soviet fundamental research and the devising and applying of techniques in industry. One reason for this has been the great prestige and material rewards of scientists. A professor-academician is at the very top of the social and income ladder. Consequently, the cream of scientific brain power tends to go into fundamental research rather than into applied science. By contrast, in the United States a successful scientist would make much more money working for a major corporation than he would pursuing an academic career. But another factor is the effect of the present Soviet planning system in discouraging innovation. This assertion would seem to contradict the widespread publicity given in the USSR for rewards for inventors, and indeed certain inventions are rewarded, especially those which receive the blessing of the central authorities.

But it is not for nothing that satirical stories abound commenting on the difficulties facing the inventor of some new design or technique. 15/ One essential weakness is lack of material inducement at enterprise level to adopt a new design or a new production layout. It is always easier to avoid the risk involved in the adoption of something new, and to proceed in the old way until ordered to do otherwise. The mental climate is especially uncongenial to inventions which, though economically desirable, do not fit in with the mystique of the grandiose. Thus Krokodil printed a little tale of the man who perfected a button-sewing machine for the clothing trade. He was told to stop bothering people with button-sewing in an age of sputniks.

Another difficulty has already been referred to: that of making the economic calculations necessary if one is to determine the advantage of using this or that machine. This is intimately connected with the entire question of price policy and economic criteria generally. The economists and planners of the bloc countries must somehow devise ways of adapting their system to the encouragement of rational innovation. At present, it is all too easy to cite examples of lopsided and unreasonable developments. 16/ But it has so far been beyond the wit of Soviet man to fit such considerations into Marxist orthodoxy.

In so far as the backwardness of the past has been due to shortage of skills, the ambitious programs of technical education must be expected to improve matters. These will also provide an increasing reservoir of skill which can be made available to assist underdeveloped countries. Already this form of aid is playing a significant role in Soviet relations with these countries. Its importance is likely to increase with the years. In this connection, the relatively elementary nature of some Soviet machinery represents an advantage, in that it is more suitable for the "beginner" in industrialization than some of the more sophisticated products of Western technology. Then, as has been pointed out elsewhere, there is no difficulty in recruiting volunteers for overseas employment, since this represents an otherwise unavailable opportunity to travel abroad and probably also a higher living standard, whereas American experts are apt to require much higher rewards to induce them to travel. It is unnecessary to make sinister assumptions about Russian technicians abroad. The bulk of them are quite harmless, and are engaged in neither subversion nor propaganda. However, the psychological effect of their very existence can be profound, and, whether or not the technicians themselves engage in political activity, one can be sure that the fact of their presence will be utilized by Soviet propaganda.

In assessing the prospects of Soviet technological advance, it is not sufficient simply to project the patchy performance of the past into the future. This may well lead us to a comfortable but ill-based optimism. Not only will the great educational effort yield dividends, but the specifically "Stalinist" features of the economy, which so discouraged innovation at ground level, should gradually be replaced by more flexible forms.

Within science itself, there is now no disposition to tolerate the oppression of the Lysenkos of the profession, although Lysenko himself has again been receiving some party support. It is no longer necessary to claim that Russians invented everything, and there is a much greater disposition to meet and discuss with Western experts. The considerable scientific brain power of the European satellites is no longer compelled to pretend that all leadership in their subjects comes from Russia. All this greater intellectual and organizational flexibility is of recent date. Stalin has not been long dead. Of course, many difficulties and restrictions remain. Nonetheless, there should be more scope for the expression of original ideas and more inducements for their effective application.

The Communist type of mind is bound to react positively to the opportunities presented by automation, and it will be the ambition of the party leadership as well as of the scientists that the USSR should be in the forefront of the so-called technological revolution of the twentieth century. In some Western countries the attitude of organized labor is an obstacle, but no such obstacle exists in Communist countries (partly because of lack of any genuine labor organizations, partly because there really is very little fear of unemployment).

One cannot pretend to forecast the course of scientific progress, but we must be prepared for rapid improvements in technique in bloc countries, and there is no reason why they should astonish us only in weapons and sputniks.

Chapter Four

BLOC PROSPECTS AND THE UNCOMMITTED WORLD

INTRODUCTION

So far, we have been considering the various factors which govern the competitive power of the bloc countries. In this section of the paper, the object will be to express some general thoughts about the bloc's economic growth and its impact in the uncommitted world. This must involve a great deal of speculation -- in the nature of things, there can be no definite "answer" to the kind of questions which must now be put. All that is possible is an attempt to take into account the relevant facts and to make a series of what are hoped to be intelligent deductions from them.

BLOC GROWTH

In the preceding sections there was a general review of the various factors affecting growth: politico-ideological, physical, and organizational. The USSR has set itself (or has been set by Khrushchev) the task of overtaking American output on a per capita basis by 1972, or even by 1970, while China has launched an industrialization drive of a unique character and pace. The Soviet seven-year plan (1959-65) enables one to make some more detailed assessment of the prospect of Soviet growth in the light of its declared objectives.

The seven-year plan provides for an annual growth rate for industry of 8.6 percent, against a rate of 10.5 percent envisaged in the abandoned sixth five-year plan (1956-60), and 13 percent claimed for the period 1951-55. The commodity targets set out in Appendix Table 2 show how ambitious the present plan is. Nonetheless, the reduction in the annual growth rate reflects a realization in Moscow that an attempt to maintain a higher pace would lead to intolerable strains, especially as this seven-year period will include some dramatic and, from the point of view of growth, expensive measures designed to satisfy the citizens' most urgent demands. National income is to increase at about 7.2 percent per annum, and agricultural output by 8 percent (by 70 percent in the seven years).

How does this rate of progress relate to the task of overtaking America? According to a semiofficial Soviet calculation, 1/ the USSR in 1955 had an industrial output 47.6 percent of that of the United States. It would seem that the Soviet leaders now consider that they are a little over half-way to American levels. 2/ If this were so, then, at 8.6 percent per annum, the USSR should reach the present level of American industrial output in 1965. Perhaps they imagine that the more rapid increase in the labor force after the mid-sixties should enable them to speed up the growth rate so as to overtake by 1970 the level which the United States will then have reached. This, anyway, is Khrushchev's declared aim, along with the achievement of the shortest hours and the "highest standard of living in the world." Already in 1965, according to the plan document, the entire Soviet bloc will produce more than half of the world's industrial output, with far-reaching political consequences on a world scale.

It now appears that the various Soviet claims are constructed on an extremely inadequate statistical base. Thus it seems from the evidence of academician Strumilin that the conclusion that Soviet industrial output is over half that of the United States is based on a ten-commodity sample, although, as he points out, "no reason is given why these ten products can replace the dynamics of the level of total industrial production of the countries being compared." 3/ There are good grounds for supposing that the gap between American and Soviet industrial production is greater than this, and for treating the claims for the future (notably "the highest standard of living in the world") with considerable skepticism, even while not denying the fact of rapid growth rates. However, before expressing views on the future, it is necessary to pause and consider what we know about the past and the present.

WHAT WAS THE RATE OF GROWTH?

The lack of a reliable official index* has stimulated many Western scholars to produce alternative calculations of the growth rates of national income and industrial production. It is impossible to analyse or list these fully. Readers must be referred to the works of G. Grossman, D. Hodgman, N. Jasny, W. Nutter, and F. Seton; also, to Colin Clark and Julius Wyler, among others, as well as to a valuable summary of the various calculations by M. C. Kaser. 4/ All agree that the official index is enormously exaggerated. They are by no means unanimous in their own conclusions, however. The lowest growth rate is that calculated by Nutter, the highest is by Seton. Table 10 illustrates the disparities.

Part of the differences are attributable to different choices of base-year weights. However, apart from difficulties in finding and justifying suitable weights, certain major obstacles stand in the way of all recalculations, of which the following are particularly important:

1. Lack of some essential data. This applies particularly to the metal goods sector. No output series can be reconstructed for many implements, instruments, many kinds of machines, ships, aircraft, armaments, and most nonferrous metals. If, as is claimed by a Soviet writer, "machine-building represents 42 percent by value of industrial output," 5/ the extent of items unknown is very substantial.

---

* Detailed remarks on the "reliability" of Soviet statistics could not be incorporated in the study for lack of space. These remarks are available as a monographed appendix free of charge upon request from NPA.

Table 10

Industrial Output Indices, USSR, 1937, 1950, 1955
(1928 = 100)

	1937	1950	1955
Nutter a/	253	376	547
Jasny b/	287	470	775
Hodgman (large-scale ind.) c/	371	646	-
Shimkin d/	275	435	715
Seton e/	380	733	1,210
Official	446	1,119	2,069

a/ Moving weights. This is the one of several indices which Nutter himself uses to compare his calculations with those of others. The use of 1928
weights gives a higher, 1955 weights a lower index. These figures are
quoted by kind permission of Dr. Nutter from his personal and yet unpub-
lished calculations. They are provisional and subject to revision.
b/ Indices of Soviet Industrial Production, 1928-59 (Council for Economic
and Industry Research), to 1950. To this has been added his estimate of
increase to 1955 in International Affairs, January 1959.
c/ Soviet Industrial Expansion, 1928-51, Harvard University Press, Cambridge, Mass., 1954.
d/ Automotive Industries, January 1, 1958.
e/ Soviet Industrial Expansion, Manchester Statistical Society, 1957.

2. Some data are known, but are not meaningful for index purposes.
Thus tons of metallurgical equipment cannot be used as a true measure of
volume change, and the same applies to meters of cloth. Some important
commodities, such as woven clothing or furniture, are available only in
money terms.

3. New products have often been given an arbitrary and excessive
weight by Soviet statisticians, but the attempt to replace this by one of our
own devising is necessarily imperfect. What, for example, is the correct
"1926/7" weight for excavators if none were made in 1926/7?

These and other difficulties have led to serious disparities even when
the same physical output series are being used. Thus Shimkin states that
his index is derived from output data compiled by the National Bureau of
Economic Research and which are the foundation of Nutter's index. Nonetheless, his index (with 1934 weights) substantially exceeds even Nutter's
1928-weighted index, though the reverse should be the case. Clearly, the
two men have made different assumptions about the behavior of the substantial sector of the economy on which adequate information is not available.

Seton's index bypasses these difficulties by being derived from steel
and energy alone, by studying the ratios of total output to steel and energy
output as shown in the growth statistics of a variety of other countries. 6/
The problem here is whether these relationships would also hold for the
Soviet Union. While a case can be made out for a somewhat lower ratio, a
large gap between Seton's index and the others should give serious cause

for reflection. Why should the relationship of industrial output to steel and energy production be so very different in the USSR to what it was elsewhere? Nutter's index in particular is highly vulnerable to such an analysis. Indeed, Nutter's understandable anxiety to combat the myth represented by the official Soviet index leads him into a position near to that of making a "myth" of rapid Soviet growth itself, an attitude which encourages a quite unwarranted degree of complacency.

A possible crosscheck, highly imperfect but not useless, suggests itself as a possible guide. Several calculations exist of the ratio of Russian to American industrial output in 1913, and the answer comes to about 9:1. 7/ If this is acceptable as an approximate "base," growth can be roughly deduced from the relative position of Soviet to American industry in 1955. As mentioned before, the Soviet claim that the USSR's output was 47.6 percent of the United States' at this date can be rejected, the more so as it appears to be based on an absurdly inadequate commodity sample. Forty percent is possible, but some would take as little as 25 percent, though anything less than a third is hard to defend. If, in 1955, Soviet industrial production were roughly a third of America's, then, since American industrial output multiplied about 4.5 times since 1913, the implied growth of Soviet industry is 13.5-fold in the period 1913-55, or roughly 12-fold in 1928-55, or the same as Seton's index. No precision is claimed for the above method, and one cannot pretend that it evades the index-number problem. However, it is not meaningless. It makes nonsense of the official Soviet claim, but also casts doubt on some of the more "conservative" Western calculations.

The relevance of calculations of the past to the present study is this: It is desirable to try to identify a trend line, and to relate to it the plans and possibilities of the future. One cannot speak of a slowdown without being able to answer the implied question: slowdown from what?

This in turn raises the very awkward question of finding a "normal" period of Soviet economic growth. Conditions have been anything but normal. Paralysis and chaos developed in 1918-21, with output a small fraction of that of 1913. The period 1921-28 was one of very quick recovery. Then came the rapid growth of industry associated with the first two five-year plans (1928-37), accompanied by the collectivization disaster in agriculture (1930-33) and recovery from this disaster. After 1937 war preparations and probably also the great purge disrupted economic advance. 8/ Then came the war itself, with all its losses of people and of capital assets. Then another period of rapid recovery, which probably was still influencing output statistics in 1951.

At the cost of stirring up some criticism, it seems not unreasonable to take the period 1951-55, extend it as far as possible to 1958, and base our future appraisal upon it, not by projecting the 1951-58 rate into the future, but rather by using it as a basis for comparison, as a period of relative normality, insofar as this word has any meaning at all.

For 1951-55, so far as industrial production is concerned, there is a strong concensus of opinion: Jasny, Shimkin and Seton all show increases by 65 percent in the five years, or 10.5 percent per annum; Nutter is odd man out with 45 percent (8 percent per annum). There is some disagreement so far as national income indices are concerned. Dr. Jasny argues for an annual growth rate of "close to 9 percent per annum" in 1951-55, while G. Grossman, in his testimony before the Joint Economic Committee of Congress, put it at 6-7 percent per annum, though this seems somewhat on the low side. All these estimates are well below the official claims, which, for the period 1951-58, are as follows (growth, annual rate of percentage increase):

	1951-5	1956	1957	1958
National income	11	12	6	9
Industrial production	13.1	11	10	10

Accepting the majority view for 1951-55, and allowing for a reasonable discount from the official claims for subsequent years, one arrives at a rough estimate of a growth rate of 9.5 percent per annum in industry for the period 1951-58, with a tendency to some slowing down in the last years of the period. National income estimates present even greater difficulty, depending greatly on the relative weights given to agriculture and services, and a wise writer does well to avoid committing himself to any figure whatsoever. Making no pretense at precision, and basing oneself on Dr. Jasny (who, given his record of searching analysis, is unlikely to be overkind to Soviet statistical claims), there is a fairly good case for an annual increase in national income of 8-8.5 percent per annum for 1951-58, with the more rapid rise in agricultural production in the last few years offsetting the decline in the growth of industry.

GROWTH PROSPECTS, 1959-65 AND THEREAFTER

If there is so much doubt and legitimate disagreement about what has already happened, it will be readily understood that there can be neither certainty nor unanimity about the yet unknown future. It is only possible to express a view in general terms. The Soviet plan for 1959-65 provides for growth of both industrial output and national income at rates much lower than those claimed for the period 1951-58, and lower also than the above estimates for the actual growth rates in this period. The factors which tend to inflate the reporting of the past are largely irrelevant to plans for the future, and there is thus no reason for not taking the official indexes of future growth as correctly expressing intention. Therefore it follows that a real slowdown is admitted -- unless one accepts the much lower Nutter estimates of past growth -- and also that the slowdown is much less pronounced than appears from the exaggerated official claims for past years. 9/

This, it must be emphasized, is only a slowdown in percentage rate, not in absolute increase. For example, an 8 percent increase in steel output now represents more steel than did a 12 percent increase ten years ago. The Soviet official statisticians are emphasizing this, understandably enough, and they further make the point that the physical increase in the output of most principal commodities now exceeds that of the United States, whereas in past years it was often true that the large increases achieved by the USSR in percentage terms left them as far, or further, behind America in terms of tons. While all this does not make the decline in rates of growth any less real, it must nonetheless be kept in mind, if unjustified complacency is to be avoided. Then, of course, it is true that the "slower" rates laid down by the Soviet planners for 1959-65--8.6 percent per annum for industry, 8 percent for agriculture, and over 7 percent for national income--are very high rates. Can they be achieved?

There is strong evidence for supposing that the special circumstances which have contributed to high growth rates in the past are becoming less effective, and the Soviet planners may not have made sufficient allowance for this. One such factor was the imposition of priorities, the ruthless concentration on the growth-inducing heavy industry. We have seen that these priorities have been modified, and it seems very doubtful whether they can be changed back again. In Chapter Two, we have already discussed in some detail other factors likely to make some slowing down of growth rates inevitable. Among these are: the heavy expenditures required for given amounts of raw-materials utilizations and agricultural production; a relative shortage of labor, leading to greater relative reliance on increased productivity; and more limited gains resulting from borrowing Western techniques. Some would add that the growth of the Soviet economy itself renders a slowdown certain, because past tempos were due to some considerable extent to the low starting point and the relative backwardness of the USSR. This, however, is not a conclusive argument. To the extent to which it is relevant, it would seem to be already subsumed among the other factors listed -- such as exhaustion of readily accessible materials, or of reserves of underemployed labor.

Against these arguments, several more "favorable" points need to be set. The educational efforts will pay dividends, both in improving the quality of the labor force and in stimulating and facilitating the development of new technique. Soviet planning, with its great opportunities for standardization and assured long runs, may prove very suitable for the development of automation. Automation will also be facilitated by the absence of organized opposition, especially on the part of workers' organization, and by the ideological predisposition of the Soviet leadership to devote resources and capital to its development. The rich natural resources of Siberia, though calling for big initial investments, may eventually pay off handsomely with substantial increases in low-cost output.

It may be argued that in some sectors -- notably agriculture -- the switch from coercion to incentives will continue to yield very favorable results, and that the stimulation of local initiative under recent reorganizations will also have a positive effect. While no one would deny that labor has become less abundant, it could be argued that the many pockets of inefficient and lavishly used labor in the economy were due to the coexistence of such abundance with the introduction of modern machinery (which, given the abundance of labor and low wages, would not have been profitable in any "capitalist" country). Consequently, as labor becomes scarcer, there are considerable hidden reserves to draw upon. The immediate shortage, due to the low wartime births, will only last for a few years.

It would be absurd to pretend that these and other factors can be systematically "weighted" and combined into a formula which entitles us to make a "scientific" projection of growth rates. So much is necessarily unknown, and one must also remind oneself that the "political stability" assumption is itself somewhat hazardous. Thus, Hungarian growth rates were seriously affected by the events of 1956, and the fantastic effort demanded of the Chinese people could well bring about a situation in which a slowdown was the only alternative to an internal explosion.

What, then, can we expect in the next seven years? Has the seven-year plan, as it stands, allowed sufficiently for the inevitable slowdown? On the whole, the balance of the evidence suggests, but by no means definitely, that the real rate of increase in industrial output may well be below the projected 8.6 percent per annum. The word "real" needs to be emphasized, because the rate officially claimed is very likely considerably to exceed 8.6 percent. Indeed, we are now (June 1959) witnessing what looks like the beginning of a campaign to fulfill the seven-year plan ahead of schedule. This may be a reflection of a belief in the existence of untapped reserves.

It is significant in this connection that Strumilin, in Literaturnaya Gazeta, (December 2, 1958), criticizes the investment program for being too large in relation to the growth rate expected; he seems to suspect chronic overbidding for investment funds on the part of the regional and functional authorities, and evidently the leadership agrees with him, since this latest campaign lays great stress on minimizing new construction and expanding output in existing factories through re-equipment and redeployment, thereby saving investment resources. Or it may herald a return to what Dr. Jasny has aptly called "hurrah-planning," which may be connected with the replacement of Kuzmin by Kosygin at the head of Gosplan early in 1959. Despite this official optimism, a genuine rate of 8.6 percent per annum should prove difficult to maintain, though 8 percent is by no means excluded. If a "guesstimate" is required, 7-8 percent seems about right. Anything above or below this range looks more unreasonable than anything within it.

In the case of agricultural output, it is necessary to make a much larger reduction in the overoptimistic official plans. The intended rate of about 8 percent per annum is quite unprecedented, even in the years of rapid recovery from Stalin's neglect. The period of diminishing returns has set in, or will very shortly do so; nor can one assume the continuance of the unusually favorable weather conditions of 1958. A rise by 4 percent per annum would be a solid achievement, and certainly seems more likely than the fulfillment of the official plan. Five percent would be remarkable. Anything above this seems practically impossible. Such a rate of progress would be consistent with a rise in national income at a rate gravitating around 6 percent per annum, though here again we can be sure that more will be claimed.

As for the period after 1965, the tendencies towards a slowdown should be counteracted by two factors working the other way: an acceleration in the rate of increase of the labor force, and the drawing of "dividends" from the long-term investment efforts now being made in East Siberia. Therefore there are no economic grounds for expecting any further slowdown in growth in the period 1965-72. Some would even argue for an acceleration during this period, though this is doubtful for political-social reasons.

Progress in the developed satellites is likely to be somewhat slower than this, in China very much faster. It is extremely hazardous to say anything useful about Chinese growth rates at present, in view not only of the remarkable (and often incredible) statistical claims 10/ and the drastic nature of social changes still in progress. But, if public order is maintained, it does seem as if the pace of Soviet development is likely to be surpassed by a wide margin. 11/

Clearly, such progress would constitute a formidable challenge. The official aim of reaching the present industrial output of the United States by 1965 seems outside the bounds of practical possibility, the more so as the USSR is not (as is claimed) already past the half-way mark. However, even the achievement by that date of three quarters of the present American level would be serious enough, and such an achievement is all too likely. This, of course, would still leave America well ahead, to an extent dependent on American growth. It would also mean that "overtaking America" either per capita or in absolute terms by 1970, in industrial production, is not a practicable aim. On the other hand, agricultural production in the USSR is already over two thirds of America's and may well supass it by 1965, the more so as the problem in the United States is the restriction rather than the stimulation of farm output. In any event, the relative growth in the economic might of the Soviet bloc will be impressive, even while it will not reach the absolute and relative levels described in the more optimistic passages of the campaign speeches of the Soviet leaders.

THE STANDARD OF LIFE

How far will Soviet growth affect living standards? Clearly, part of the potential appeal of the Soviet system would reside in its ability to demonstrate the achievement of more prosperity for the citizens. It does not follow that even a spectacular increase in the national product and in industrial production must lead to higher living standards. Thus in the early period of Soviet industrialization there was a rise in national income and a very big increase in aggregate industrial production, accompanied by a drastic fall in the standard of living of both workers and peasants. Even today, while Soviet national income is many times higher than in 1928, the purchasing power of the average wage has increased relatively little.

There are several explanations of this state of affairs. One is the statistical effect of urbanization. A peasant, especially in a subsistence economy, "generates" much less national income at a given level of consumer satisfaction than does the same peasant once he migrates to town. In town, many processes formerly carried out within a peasant household are commercialized and so find their way into the national accounts without thereby increasing welfare. The urban citizen requires many more services. It is inevitable, therefore, that urbanization should itself cause a large rise in the national income and in the measurable output of consumers' goods and services. 12/

Another essential explanation lies in the great increase in the share of producers' goods in total output, and of services rendered to industry in the total of services rendered. This is in part a universal phenomenon: There is evidence that the greater complexity of industry leads to some increase in the relative importance of producers' goods in all the major industrial countries. But this tendency has been accentuated in the USSR and in other bloc countries by deliberate state policy, and the same has been true of services.

All this is very relevant to the developments which are likely to occur in China. We will probably see some very striking increases in national income and industrial production in China, even if (as is quite likely) the process of ultra-rapid industrialization is associated with static (or even declining) living standards. However, the situation of the USSR and of the developed satellites is quite different. They are already largely industrialized, and face the necessity of making some effort to improve the living standards. In part, as has already been argued, this necessity arises from internal social pressures; in part, it relates to the external policies of the bloc. Thus the USSR itself has for long been conscious of the impact of such towns as Tashkent and Alma Ata, and of the relatively prosperous cotton-growing farms of Central Asia, 13/ on visitors from other Asian countries.

We must expect a genuine increase in the standard of life in those countries of the Soviet bloc which have already passed through the stages of "primitive accumulation," and the plans of the USSR and of the major European satellites all show a marked preoccupation with improvements in the way of life of their citizens. It would indeed be very foolish of us to hold the crude propaganda-poster view that the leadership is merely a collection of power-hungry thugs who totally neglect the citizens. To admit that the Communist chiefs are interested in welfare does not, of course, imply any kind of moral approbation. More than one dictator has taken much trouble to clothe, feed, and pay his peoples and, indeed, this is usually best from his point of view. Farmers have been known to feed their animals well, too, without wishing to give them votes. We should accept as a fact that an effort is being made markedly to improve the low living standards of the USSR and of such countries as East Germany, Czechoslovakia, and Poland. Khrushchev's seven-year plan theses show that he is very conscious of the political value of more welfare: The effort seems to be quite real.

The extent of the real improvement must depend on a number of factors. One is progress of agriculture, to which extensive reference has already been made. Another depends on the determination with which the promised campaigns to improve housing and industrial consumers' goods production are carried through. At present it does appear as if a fairly high priority is being given to these sectors. But there remains another and more serious difficulty, connected with the nature of the system itself. Neither in theory nor in practice is the system adapted to the satisfaction of consumers' wants. While certainly able, if appropriate decisions are taken, to increase production of cotton cloth, toothbrushes or frying pans, the system responds clumsily -- if it responds at all -- to the ever-changing pattern of demand. The Marxist theory of value fails to recognize the role of demand, and the price system fails to "transmit" to the producers the requirements of the consumers -- except in the unhelpful sense that a useless good has no value and a totally unsalable article is not worth producing.

The outlawing of private trading and strict limitations on private services have not been replaced by effective state-organized action. In this field the profit motive is singularly hard to replace. In so far as local authorities are responsible for welfare, 14/ the fact that they are not truly elected deprives the population of an effective means of pressure upon their "representatives." These weaknesses do not seem curable within the existing political and economic system. Yet, above a certain level, increases in living standards involve not so much the consumption of more basic products but, more precisely, improvements in quality, finer adjustments to what people really prefer, and the provision of more services. Here the advanced countries of the West are several generations ahead of the USSR.

There is really no prospect whatever of the USSR overtaking the West in the field of living standards. Over time, of course, the lag should diminish gradually. Developed countries like Czechoslovakia already compare very favorably with such a poor "Western" country as Italy. China, on the other hand, may be pressing down her very modest living standards in the effort to build a great industry in the shortest time. The USSR, with gradual improvements in the appalling housing conditions, genuinely impressive social services and increased variety in the shops, will be able to make a better impression on visitors from the poorer countries of the world, and the impression will be the greater because these countries believe that Russia was once as poor as they are now, and that she has lifted herself up by her own bootstraps. This belief is politically significant.

COHESION OF THE BLOC

So far nothing has been said about relationships within the bloc. It may be asked: Are these countries likely to work harmoniously together, and will they be able to concert their policies?

This is in large part a political question, affected by possible conflicts of interest between Russia and China, the fate of "revisionist" and national-communist tendencies in Poland, and so on -- factors which are beyond the scope of the present paper. However, it would be wrong to suppose that intrabloc economic collaboration and political subordination are necessarily directly related to one another. Thus in the last Stalin years, the maximum political subordination of the satellites to the Soviet Union was accompanied by very little economic coordination. There was, it is true, exploitation by the USSR of the weaker brethren, but joint planning remained very largely a matter of words, with little action. Since 1956, on the other hand, crude exploitation has ceased, there is more autonomy for the various countries and, paradoxically, joint long-term planning is becoming more of a reality. It is extending also into the field of trade with countries outside the bloc, although at the same time such active "traders" as Czechoslovakia and Poland apparently have a good deal of independent initiative in trade matters.

We should ask ourselves how far the cooperation between bloc countries reflects a real community of economic interest, and how far it is a matter either of political convenience or mere coercion. These questions are of much more than theoretical interest. Thus if the bloc countries only work together in the economic field because of orders from Moscow, it follows that any weakening in Soviet dominance should be expected to lead to strong centrifugal tendencies with all that this implies. No doubt the satellites wish to avoid their own exploitation. The problem is whether there is a basis for voluntary cooperation.

There are a number of points which must be taken into account in this connection. First of all, these regimes are led by Communists, and this not only inclines them to cooperation, but involves them in programs of ambitious economic growth and in basing their economic life on planning. This, in turn, has certain consequences. Planning authorities everywhere like to plan well ahead, to minimize risks. Clearly, this would incline them towards long-term deals with other centrally planned economies, even if there were no political uncertainties. But there are political uncertainties, which in the economic field may express themselves in politically motivated trade embargoes, or in the imposition of restrictive quotas. The cold war is a reality which central planners can hardly overlook. Therefore the tendency favorable to intrabloc deals is powerfully reinforced.

Still another factor of a much less "political" kind has to be considered. 15/ The European satellites are dependent for their existence on imports of raw materials and, in many cases, of food, and it is clear that earnings of foreign exchange are among the principal limiting factors which restrict economic growth. The planners and economists of Poland, East Germany, and Czechoslovakia, are acutely aware of this. They must seek markets. But these countries have little to sell apart from manufactures (Polish coal and perhaps Rumanian oil are the only major exceptions). Their best chance is to export machinery. But where to? In the "world market" they find tough competition from the major industrial powers. Underdeveloped countries, especially those whose financial or political status is uncertain, provide a possible market, of which more will be said later; but they cannot suffice. Russia and China, on the other hand, offer enormous opportunities. Already they are among the world's biggest importers of machinery, and are likely to be safe long-term markets. The bulk of their machinery imports are supplied by the developed satellites. In return, the USSR and China can supply many of the necessary materials. It is true that some of these (especially minerals) are inconveniently located and involve heavy transportation costs. Nonetheless, there is real economic logic in using the skill of Central Europe to process raw materials for the Russo-Chinese.

This logic has been hidden from our view for two reasons. One is the unreasonable behavior of the planners of these countries. In the words of Professor Lange, 16/ each of the countries of the bloc sought to do everything for itself and to make itself "a little replica of the Soviet Union." He cited the Hungarian steel industry as a prime example. The other is the element of exploitation. Obviously, no transaction can ever look right or rational if it is concluded at revolver point, or if one side imposes unfair prices upon the other. But it does not at all follow from this that mutually profitable deals are impossible. On the contrary, they seem quite possible on a large scale, and may already be decisive for the industrialized satellites.

The logic of these developments calls insistently for joint long-term planning, which has so far been almost nonexistent. The satellites have few natural advantages as industrial countries. There are hardly any types of machinery which could not be produced in any of them or in Russia itself. In the absence of "natural" specialization, there is much to be said for deliberate decisions about investment, so as to avoid wasteful duplication.

48

Thus the USSR may refrain from expanding her inadequate capacity to produce railroad equipment, on the understanding that East Germany and Poland will supply her needs. Some of the results are reflected in an article by the Soviet economist Bogomolov. He listed a number of agreements about specialization in producing machinery and equipment, and referred to some long-term trade plans -- for example, Soviet oil exports to East Germany in 1965 are expected to be 4.8 million tons, against 1 million in 1957; Soviet sales of iron ore to Czechoslovakia are expected to reach 10.1 million tons, against 3.6 million tons in 1958.

Apart from arrangements through the Council for Mutual Economic Assistance, 17/ the USSR held bilateral talks with all "socialist countries" concerning planning and trade coordination for the period 1959-65. A map shows pipelines from Soviet oilfields into Poland, East Germany, and Hungary. 18/ The remarkable thing is not that the bloc is coordinating its economic planning, but only that this has begun so very recently. The joint machinery within CMEA is still clumsy and is inevitably hamstrung by the centralization, within each of the countries, of basic economic decisions. Thus it took a gathering of supreme party bosses in Moscow in May 1958 to launch serious coordination, and the proper routine arrangements may work none too well. It is perhaps worth noting that the plan provides for an increase in Soviet trade with the bloc smaller (50 percent) than the intended rise in national income.

Divergencies of interest must often arise, even if the USSR does not use its political position within the bloc for economic advantage. There are possible conflicts of priorities: For example, China's claims on heavy industrial equipment may be a serious burden to other bloc countries. Within the coordinating machinery, there can be strong arguments about who should specialize on what. The USSR may urge the development of some industry whose products she requires, while the domestic planners may consider that this industry is relatively uneconomic. So much depends on relative prices, and the confusion which still reigns in the domestic price pattern and foreign exchange rates of all bloc countries makes objective calculations of advantage a most uncertain thing. Another potential source of trouble is the carrying out of politically motivated deals with the underdeveloped countries and the sharing of whatever burdens such deals may impose -- more will be said about this question later on.

The Soviet bloc countries are led by Communists, but, as the example of Gomulka shows, they do not necessarily take kindly to being ordered about, and they may be presumed to be keen enough on their own national developments to resent the imposition of unfair exchanges. Therefore, great tact and self-restraint will be needed to keep the bloc working together, plus perhaps continued international tension. Otherwise, the satellites most dependent for their livelihood on international trade would surely endeavor to make deals of their own with nonbloc countries, which would commit resources needed elsewhere in the bloc. Indeed, some of them may be doing this just now; we must not imagine that every effort by any bloc country to make trade agreements and to sell its goods is part of a coordinated plan of economic warfare.

There is one aspect of intrabloc trade which calls for comment. The "underdeveloped" members of the bloc not only take a high proportion of the exportable investment goods of their industrialized fellow-members, but they find that they must pay for them very largely in foodstuffs and consumers' goods. This is most obviously so in the case of Sino-Soviet trade. 19/ On balance, the USSR supplies China with investment goods and obtains in exchange a large quantity of commodities which are not directly conducive to economic growth. The logic of bilateralism makes this inevitable, granted the determination (itself largely political in origin) to cooperate in the industrialization of China. The interesting question is: Does this delay Russian growth? The answer depends in part on what steps the Soviet authorities would have had to take to satisfy domestic consumer demand if the Chinese contribution would have been absent. If, as is quite possible, the "missing" oilseeds, meat, fruit, and textiles would have to be supplied from within the USSR (or alternative consumers' goods in their place), then the process of exchange need not affect Soviet growth and may in fact assist it. However, it remains likely that Chinese orders for machinery frequently conflict with Soviet internal needs in sectors where shortages can and do develop. Consequently, China's industrialization must impose strains, which could grow in the immediate future as the process speeds up. One can envisage disputes on these matters at the political level.

It may be significant that in 1957 there was a marked fall in Chinese imports from the USSR, leaving a large Chinese export surplus. 20/ Far from receiving Soviet aid, therefore, the Chinese would now seem to be "aiding" the USSR, and there are indications that this continued in 1958. It is true that the reason may have been the repayment by China of past credits, and the new agreement signed in Moscow during the 21st Party Congress may lead to a renewed upward trend in Soviet deliveries, especially of capital goods. On the other hand, this agreement says nothing of any Soviet aid or credits, and China appears to have undertaken to pay on current account. If this is so, then Chinese export surpluses will continue for some time yet, and the current trade balance of the USSR will be correspondingly relieved. Yet China is known to have difficulty, in the midst of the efforts and confusion of her industrial development, in keeping up her exports. Thus some commitments to western countries have not been kept in the past year. Therefore, Chinese communist leaders may well strongly press Moscow for more capital goods and for credits, or at least for a postponement of further repayments.

IMPACT ON UNDERDEVELOPED WORLD--FORCE OF EXAMPLE

There is a tendency in some quarters to view the Soviet danger too exclusively in terms of some specific actions-- military, "economic penetration," etc.--by the USSR and her allies. Yet an important part of our difficulties arise from the psychological effects of Soviet achievements on the climate of opinion in underdeveloped countries. It is important for us to realize why this is so. The alleged skill of Soviet propaganda is a quite insufficient explanation, for without fertile soil it would be as ineffective in India and Egypt as it is in West Germany or Great Britain. Nor is it very useful to react by impatiently accusing the intellectuals of the affected countries of being fools, who are wilfully blind to the superior economic achievements of the United States.

50

The situation of the bulk of the underdeveloped countries is a peculiarly difficult one. They generally wish to stimulate economic development, especially industrialization, so as to reduce poverty and to raise the status of their country in the modern world. But they face a number of obstacles:

1. The social and often also the political structure belongs to a pre-industrial age and acts as a brake on development. For instance, the few possessors of great wealth are not generally disposed to use it for productive investment. Administrative and fiscal inefficiency, corruption, the relics of feudalism -- all these are obstacles.

2. The bulk of the people are generally illiterate and politically helpless, and/or in the grip of ancient superstitions. Democratic forms, where they exist, seem quite ineffective as a means of securing changes necessary for modernization. It is like expecting a population brought up on witch-doctors to vote for modern medicine. In any event, with few exceptions, governments are manipulated by existing vested interests.

3. Industrialization of a peasant country, by methods which the West regards as normal, causes acute difficulties in the purely economic field. The beginnings of industrialization lead to a large increase in imports (for instance, of machinery and chemicals), and a continuing burden of interest on foreign loans. A growing urban population meanwhile absorbs more food and raw materials and reduces the potential exportable surplus. At the same time, the townsmen are attracted to imported manufactures not yet produced within the country. The new industries tend to be inefficient and earn little foreign currency. The result is a balance of payments crisis which painfully restricts the growth of the economy. 21/

It is apt to cite here the words of Professor Simon Kuznets: "The most serious obstacle to the rapid spread of the industrial system is one which it shares with many major innovations: it means a marked break in established patterns of social and economic life; it destroys established interests; it requires a system of social values and a cultural milieu quite different from those which are the heritage of a long historical past in many countries. In short it is a thoroughgoing revolution, in the full sense of the word." 22/ It is in this context that the political appeal and the force of Russia's example must be seen. This is why gradualist or conservative proposals tend to be regarded as affording no solution to the country's problems.

For all these reasons, thoughtful men in underdeveloped countries are often predisposed towards radical, revolutionary solutions, and see no hope in gradualism. Democracy means little to them, respect for existing interests or for existing popular prejudices appears to be the negation of progress. Russia, they argue, was one of us, and has become a great industrial power. In the process, whole classes have been liquidated and the masses pushed around, but this may well seem inevitable and necessary to the radicals of these countries. Development involves sacrifice. Sacrifice requires not only coercion but also a purpose. Totalitarian ideologies therefore have their attractions for these people. All this does not necessarily lead the reformers to become Communists; but it does lead to impatience with old ways, a willingness to listen to extremists, a desire to study what Russia has done and what China is doing. The experience of Western countries seems simply irrelevant: Their social and economic situation was and is totally different, and their experience cannot be applied.

All this gives the Soviet bloc a strong psychological-political advantage, even if no "penetration" of the familiar kind is occurring. The political advantage is much enhanced by actions of the West when, with immediate strategic aims in mind, we underpin the existing regimes in many of these countries. Thus the reformers may feel that their government relies on American dollars to maintain itself and to stave off internal reforms which would otherwise be inevitable. Russians do not fail to point out that there is no tyrant so bloodthirsty and so obscurantist who would not be supported by the United States, provided he took the correct anti-Soviet posture. Unfortunately, this is also known to the enemies of reform, who accordingly bid for dollar aid in the guise of anticommunism -- and sometimes tend to spend these dollars on conspicuous consumption (luxury automobiles), rather than on making their economies viable, often to the dismay of American economic advisers.

This line of argument is not intended to imply that the USSR is a constant supporter of "progress." Indeed, it is not unwilling to back old-fashioned tyrants if it suits its purposes (for instance, in the Yemen). The point is rather that the economic achievements of Communist countries are peculiarly impressive to many citizens of underdeveloped countries, that the coercion which accompanied the achievements does not seem shocking in the light of their own experience, and that the apparent alliance between anti-progressives in their own countries and the United States helps Soviet propagandists considerably.

The achievement of economic progress by the noncommunist road, and by such a country as India, would greatly influence the situation. In India herself, and among her neighbors, the comparison is made between India and China. Starting together at a very low level, their relative growth is widely regarded as a test between systems. In this connection, it is important to ensure that false or distorted statistics are clearly shown to be such. The USSR, for instance, lays claim to a long-term growth rate which is quite unique, whereas, properly deflated, it may well be little higher than that of Japan in the period 1900-40 (to cite an outstanding example). Japan's story, indeed, should be much better known, for clearly its remarkable features owe nothing to Communist ideas and it was, too, a backward, peasant and an Asian country.

The Soviet Union's collectivization of agriculture is frequently seen by Asian intellectuals as a model relevant to their needs. In their own countries, agriculture is generally handicapped by social, legal, and technical patterns which urgently require change, and Soviet collective farming is often regarded as a progressive form of rural cooperation. The real nature of Soviet collectivization is seldom appreciated, and it is surely the duty of Western scholars and propagandists to make it known. But the need to reform drastically the agriculture of these countries is urgent, and purely negative criticism of the Soviet record would probably be ineffective unless an alternative road is advocated, which is more suitable to the special needs of farming in those areas. A few, too few, Western experts are doing just that.

Finally, a brief reference is clearly necessary to the impression which Chinese growth is already making, and must increasingly make, on the minds of people in the uncommitted world, especially in Asia. The most remarkable claims are being made in industry and agriculture alike. The Chinese "rural communes" may appeal as a means of "freeing" the peasants from their traditional attitudes as well as mobilizing their labor for agricultural investment and industrial production in the villages, although the excesses of "communization" may scare off many Asian well-wishers.

Those well informed on the effects of Soviet collectivization on farm output and peasant work will note the apparent contrast which Chinese experience affords, 23/ the more so as Chinese, rather than Soviet, conditions are bound to seem more relevant to the problems faced in India or Indonesia. We may find that the Chinese model will exercise a great attraction, whether or not China disburses much aid or enters into extensive trading relations with the countries concerned. It is all the more important that those competent to judge the pace and cost of Chinese development -- of which the author of these lines is not one -- should be able to correct the exaggerations of which Chinese propaganda is likely to be guilty.

TRADE AND AID

While the indirect political effects of Soviet growth on underdeveloped countries are likely to be formidable and are frequently underestimated, the direct impact of bloc economic power on these countries is certainly important too. Unfortunately, a realistic analysis is often rendered difficult by thinking in purely political terms. Thus, as Dr. Berliner has pointed out, we tend to speak of the vastness of the Soviet "penetration" effort, and then argue that the extent of actual Soviet aid has been comparatively small, though it is hard to maintain both these positions at once. We are apt to adopt "political" explanations for all trade deals, and thereby deprive ourselves of the means of identifying those deals which really are predominantly political. There is also an unnecessary confusion at times between aid and trade.

These points are of real importance in any assessment of the situation. Aid is seldom given by anyone on grounds of pure philanthropy. It implies some degree of sacrifice on the part of the bloc, and obviously the decision to make this sacrifice is related to a more or less precise anticipation of political advantage, whereas trade relations generally involve no sacrifice at all (on the contrary, they should yield some net economic gain), unless the deal is entered into on purely political grounds. All this implies that there are two problems here: First, what economic burdens is the bloc likely to shoulder in its relations with the underdeveloped world? And, second, what mutually advantageous trading relationships are rendered possible by the needs of the various countries?

It may be objected that there is quite a large field in which motivation is mixed. For instance, the USSR purchases more fish from Iceland and cocoa from Ghana, ceases to purchase oranges from Israel and buys no bananas, though the Soviet internal trade network needs all these commodities. There is room for political maneuver, and the satisfaction of this or that internal need may be decided by political considerations. Indeed, the entire decision to reverse Stalinist isolationism and enter more widely into world trade was based, no doubt, on a calculation into which politics entered prominently. Nonetheless, it would be foolish to speak of Soviet Russia's suffering an economic loss from such deals. The Soviet consumer must be enabled to spend his rubles, inflation must be combated, and it seems quite probable that the extra fish and cocoa were welcome to the Soviet planners and represented a net gain.

One should not overlook the tendency of Soviet publicists always to emphasize the political aspect of any of their transactions, and indeed to imply that aid is given when there is in fact no net aid at all. One need only recall the claims made for the USSR's altruistic help to her European satellites, which were made at a time when these countries were being severely exploited by the Soviet Union. Many commentators misunderstood the announcement, in 1959, concerning Soviet deliveries of factories to China; it was made to look like "aid," even though it is all to be paid for and no credits seem to be involved. Even in internal Soviet planning, the political origin and purpose of technical-economic decisions are generally overstressed in Soviet official statements. In taking these statements too literally, we sometimes unnecessarily help Soviet propaganda. They have not, in fact, sacrificed much; net aid, properly deflated and analyzed, has been of modest dimensions, and the strain on the bloc economies is all the smaller if arms are left out of account, for these are likely to be surpluses, which it is unnecessary to replace.

It has become customary in the West to stress the vast extent of Soviet aid to underdeveloped countries, the object being partly to dramatize the nonmilitary dangers to the West, and partly to persuade reluctant congressmen to vote foreign aid programs. An impressive total is generally quoted and it is true that the total has by now risen to about $2.5 billion, including Yugoslavia. 24/ The precise makeup of this total is uncertain, since the data are not systematically published and require to be reconstructed. Table 11 presents an estimated breakdown by principal countries of the above total.

This total is often compared with American or total Western aid to underdeveloped countries. Yet this is misleading for the following reasons:

First, this total represents a sum of promises, over a period of three or four years, and only partly of loans actually made or credits actually granted. The credits will be gradually drawn upon during the next few years. So far, out of the above impressive total, at the most only $750 million has actually been disbursed.

Second, the sum is gross of actual repayments made by the recipient countries. Egypt and Burma, for instance, have been running large export surpluses with bloc countries -- that is, they have been repaying part of their "aid" with goods. This must surely be allowed for, and makes the actual volume of aid given smaller still.

Third, nearly all Soviet aid has taken the form of interest-bearing loans. It is true that the interest rate has been below normal commercial levels, but obviously a loan cannot be compared, on a 1 to 1 basis, with a straight grant. The element of aid in a loan is only the difference between the interest rate charges and the commercial rate. Yet not only American

Table 11

Sino-Soviet Bloc Aid, January 1954 - March 1959
(Million dollars)

Egypt	620
Syria	325
Iraq	255
Yemen	50
Afghanistan	160
Burma	40
India	310
Ceylon	50
Indonesia	360
Cambodia	30
Argentina	104
All others (excl. Yugoslavia) a/	36
Total (excl. Yugoslavia)	2340
Yugoslavia	160
Total (incl. Yugoslavia)	2500

a/ Ethiopia, Iran, Turkey, Nepal, Iceland, and Brazil.

Source: Estimates, partially based on testimony by Under Secretary of State Dillon before Senate Foreign Relations Committee, reprinted in State Department Bulletin, February 9, 1959.

but also British aid has a large grant component. Indeed, even if a 1 to 1 basis were accepted, the value of grants actually made to underdeveloped countries by Great Britain alone, in the period of 1954-58, compares very favorably with the net loans actually made by the bloc. U. S. government economic aid alone, considering just the year ending June 30, 1957, amounted to $1,628 million, of which $1,342 million were outright grants, according to Berliner's careful calculations. The inclusion of military aid (which is included in the Soviet figures) would enormously increase this total, which also neglects nongovernmental and international agency aid. If all these factors are borne in mind, there might be a more realistic assessment of the scale of Soviet aid and of the extent of the burdens so far borne by the bloc.

But while net aid so far has been rather modest, the question remains whether it will not grow in the next few years. One must distinguish here between the actual flow of net credits (or rather of goods supplied on credit, less goods received in repayment) and new commitments undertaken. On the basis of existing commitments, the annual rate of Soviet deliveries should show an upward tendency. However, it is doubtful whether the rate at which new credits are negotiated will surpass (or perhaps even equal) the peak year 1956. There are two reasons for this, which, though interconnected, are logically separate. One is the commitment of bloc resources in general, and of capital equipment in particular, to maintain the bloc's own growth rates. The other is the relatively tight balance-of-payments position of most members of the bloc, including even the USSR itself, which makes "unrequited" exports unpopular with harassed planners. This would allow for the granting of more credits to a few selected countries when the political dividends are tempting. Iraq is the most recent example of such a policy, which will doubtless be continued as and when such opportunities occur.

However, Soviet bloc policy seems to be more concerned with its own growth in the long term. The strengthening of the bloc's economies is priority Number One. Opportunities will be taken when they involve commitment of relatively small resources in the hope of a big return. The extension of aid on a much larger scale than this is, of course, physically possible. Thus the above view represents an estimate of political priority, and cannot be "proved" to be correct. Certainly net aid absorbs an extremely small fraction of national income. Yet the course of policy so far supports this interpretation.

One type of aid may prove an exception, and this is technical assistance. It seems likely that technically qualified personnel will become increasingly available, and this is an effective way of rendering help, which can be given widespread publicity and costs little.

Why, then, if Soviet bloc aid is relatively so much smaller than the West's, has it had such a remarkable political effect? The following factors might be significant:

1. Novelty: a new source of capital is attractive in itself.

2. The USSR's much-advertised "anti-imperialist" reputation, and her claim not to intervene in the foreign policies of the recipients ("no strings"). This claim is not so easy to uphold now, in the face of the Soviet involvement (possibly against Soviet wishes) in the bitter Iraqi-Egyptian quarrel, although so far Soviet aid policies have not been modified as a result of Egyptian political hostility.

3. A loan at a low rate of interest may be better for the morale and self-respect of the recipient than a "charitable" grant.

4. Soviet credits tend to support the development projects put forward by the "development-minded" interests in the recipient country. They are repayable in goods, thereby easing the burden of repayments on currency -- or seeming to. Western aid is less attractive in these respects.

5. Finally, the relative size of Soviet aid programs is consistently exaggerated by the West's own propaganda, within the hearing of under-developed countries.

We may also attribute to the effect of aid the psychological impact of the Soviet example, of her growth to economic great-power status, to which extensive reference has already been made. 25/

Trade relations are another and complicated story, involving a number of potentially or actually divergent considerations. Thus the possible political and economic advantages of expanding foreign trade conflict with the long-ingrained habits of the planners, and the structure of the Soviet-type economy lacks the necessary flexibility.

The expansion of bloc trade with the underdeveloped world carries with it some very obvious political advantages. Certainly the development of economic ties gives political opportunities. It lessens dependence of these countries on the West; it has psychological-political consequences desirable from the Soviet point of view. This is particularly to the Soviet advantage if a given country has run into trouble in its relations with the West--as, for instance, was the case with Egypt and Iceland. Finally, it may lay those countries which rely heavily on their trade with the bloc open to pressures, similar to those which Germany was able to exercise in Southeast Europe in the days of Schacht. It is true that the USSR has tended to make a virtue of avoiding any political "strings," and made political capital out of this. However, the recent troubles with Yugoslavia suggest that tactical considerations will be decisive in this connection. At the same time, the example of Yugoslavia proves something else: that a country greatly dependent economically on the Soviet bloc can assert its independence, if it is determined to do so.

There are also important political advantages in expanding genuine trade with the Western countries themselves, quite apart from obvious economic benefits of such trade. Thus German or British businessmen may (so Moscow must hope) exert pressure for a less hostile policy towards Soviet Russia if they can do profitable business with her. One may ask why, while Stalin was alive, he pursued so restrictionist a policy, when it was not in the Soviet political or economic interest to do so. Presumably one answer is simply that Stalin believed in principle in the minimization of contacts with the outside world, and that this view took priority over the advantages which might have been derived from them. Khrushchev is both less morbidly suspicious and more confident. There is also a different reading of the military situation, which has been transformed by the new weapons and makes less sense of strategic self-sufficiency.

Thus from the Soviet standpoint there are strong political reasons in favor of trade expansion. To these must be added strong economic arguments, which apply to trade both with the West and with the underdeveloped world. The typical exports of many underdeveloped countries, especially those in tropical areas, consist of commodities which are either non-existent or scarce in the Soviet bloc. The USSR and many of its partners are also anxious to extend their purchases in Western countries, notably of machinery. We can be sure that at any given moment the foreign trade ministries of all bloc countries face far more requests for import author-izations than can possibly be paid for, and this problem of paying for imports appears to be the immediate limiting factor. The payments question has a much greater influence on Soviet import and export policy than is generally realized, and in 1959 this aspect of the matter has been dramatized by Soviet approaches both to the United States and to Great Britain for long-term credits.

The need to export to pay for imports surely explains many Soviet efforts to sell, which some Western critics ascribe to subtle (or even sinister) political maneuvers. Thus there is abundant evidence that the USSR was short of sterling in 1957-58, and this may well have led to great efforts to find more commodities to sell in London and elsewhere. These included additional quantities of timber (although this is a scarce commodity in Russia itself), but also tin and aluminum. Sales of these two metals have been widely interpreted as politically motivated, though these sales, and the fact that they involved a challenge to an existing price-maintenance agreement, can be logically explained in terms of a drive to earn much-needed "valuta." There is, indeed, a marked tendency -- and not only in trade matters -- to ascribe to Soviet acts a directly political motivation, when many of these acts are "technical" consequences of other decisions and are several stages removed from politics. To take an earlier historical example: Sales of Russian butter in 1930-32 were not intended (as some argued at the time) to disrupt the market by dumping; they were rendered necessary by big purchases of machinery abroad, which had to be paid for.

These purchases were, of course, a consequence of a political decision about industrialization. So, today, the aim to maximize Soviet economic might is political. In pursuit of it certain steps are necessary, among them the importation of materials and equipment from the sterling area. These have to be paid for. Russian commodities are therefore thrown on the world market. Someone is hurt, especially at a time when prices are falling anyhow. It is tempting to view Russian sales as aiming primarily to hurt for directly political reasons, but it need not be so at all in reality.

The problem posed by Soviet commodity sales remains, whatever the motivation of the sales themselves. Thus, although dumping is not undertaken for its own sake, the fact remains that Soviet sellers commonly reduce prices to whatever level is necessary to sell the product. Export availabilities, because they are seldom consciously planned far ahead, are apt to appear and disappear, as consequences of some imbalance of planned development, chance surpluses, or an unusually good or bad harvest, and this irregularity can have a disruptive effect. This could happen in the next few years with exports of grain, oil, diamonds from the USSR, motor-cycles from Czechoslovakia, or cotton textiles from China, to take a few examples at random.

The result, especially in industrialized Western countries, is to stimulate protective measures designed to keep such goods out. This can, in some circumstances, be a more effective obstacle to the growth of East-West trade than the lack of exportable surpluses of Eastern countries. Thus the USSR may wish to buy American or British machinery, but find that the goods it can sell are excluded from the United States and Great Britain. Such a situation could contribute to an export drive to Latin America or the overseas sterling area designed to earn dollars or sterling to spend in the United States or Great Britain.

It is often asked: Why do they not sell gold instead? The answer might be given in three parts. First, as their textbooks abundantly demonstrate, the Soviets take gold and gold reserves very seriously, almost like an orthodox 19th-century capitalist, and are most reluctant to run down these reserves. Second, there are some grounds for suspecting that current gold production is not as high as some Western analysts imagine, and it is quite possible that the gold they have actually sold in recent years has been roughly equal to current production. Third, in present circumstances, with the virtual end of forced labor, bearing in mind the remote Arctic location of Soviet gold mines, it seems uneconomic to mine gold for sale abroad at $35 an ounce. It would make better sense to sell other things, including tin and aluminum. Finally, they may have been hoping for a rise in the price of gold.

The economic attractiveness of trading with underdeveloped countries arises not only from the availability in these countries of commodities useful in the Soviet economy, but also from the fact that they are often a convenient market for bloc exports of a type very hard to sell elsewhere. Many countries of the bloc, including to an increasing extent the Soviet Union itself, are endeavouring to extend their export of manufactures, and especially of machinery and equipment. But where are these machines to be sold? Obviously not many can go to the West. It is also hard to sell them where Western influence is strong and Western firms predominate in the economy (for instance in the Philippines or in Venezuela). Consequently the selling effort is naturally concentrated in other underdeveloped countries, which in many cases are also politically sensitive. The granting of credits to such countries assists in the process of establishing trade links. Nevertheless a Czech or a Polish trade official would react indignantly if accused of "political trading:" "We sell where we can; where else can we sell our goods?" This official may speak quite sincerely, because political and economic advantage point the same way.

The economic basis exists for advantageous and politically attractive trading relations on a much expanded scale between the bloc and the underdeveloped world. The latter may well be attracted by the thought that the Soviet bloc does not suffer from recessions, and that there exists the possibility of firm long-term contracts. As suppliers of manufactures, there is no reason why the developed bloc countries --with their modernized industry and low wages -- should not sell at genuinely competitive prices. One difficulty which the Soviet bloc countries face in this direction is their inability to calculate comparative advantage, owing to irrational price structures and exchange rates. Another difficulty is their lack of experience in supplying specialized goods to distant customers--this has been particularly noticeable in the case of some Soviet manufactures. However, neither of these difficulties is necessarily insuperable.

Yet, despite all these political and economic advantages, the Soviet planners do not seem to have adjusted their thought processes adequately to the new situation. While trade exchanges have expanded by considerable percentages from the low levels of the late-Stalin period, they are still very largely confined, so far as the USSR is concerned, to marginal quantities. Self-sufficiency seems still to be the basic aim, and a continuing dependence on supplies from outside the bloc is still avoided. The evidence suggests that there is little planning of export surpluses in the USSR. Nor is this really surprising, bearing in mind the pressures under which Soviet planners operate. They are faced with the difficult enough task of meeting numerous and competing demands on limited resources, to ensure the fulfilment of the ambitious plans for growth. If capacity in a given industry promises to be more than sufficient to meet the expected internal demand, there is a tendency to expand some other industry where capacity is inadequate. Alternatively, plans are modified to increase the use of the given product within the USSR itself. For example, the bulk of the expected increase in grain production is intended to increase the output of meat for the Soviet home market.

If, on the other hand, there is a shortage of any commodity, the first reaction is generally to ensure that it can be supplied from within the bloc. Thus the great expansion of the chemical industry, and the consequential increases in purchases of chemical machinery from the West, may well be intended--among other things--to reduce long-term dependence on imports. All this is more noticeable in the USSR than in the European satellites; the latter must trade extensively with the outside world and do plan for such trade. It is also true that this restrictionist attitude is no longer typical of planning within the bloc, which now includes a considerable degree of usual specialization. 26/ Nonetheless, the fact that the plan does not adequately provide for foreign trade is itself an obstacle to its development.

This obstacle is not due purely to ideological and political considerations; it is also connected with the process of planning itself. Foreign trade with countries and at prices wholly beyond control injects an element of risk into the planning process. There is always the possibility that market prognostications prove faulty, that for some unforeseen reasons trade could be interrupted. It must always seem safer to base long-term plans and the investment program on more secure foundations--that is, within one's own area of political control. In addition, the bureaucratic clumsiness resulting from the centralization of foreign trade inclines local economic units and enterprises towards deals within their own countries, rather than to attempt to surmount the many structural obstacles which stand between them and the foreign customer or supplier.

Planning for much more foreign trade is within Soviet "capabilities" in the sense that there is no physical obstacle to it. But there remains an inbuilt reluctance to lean too heavily on the outside world. A contributory factor, which is an obstacle to trade, is the habit of bilateralism. This habit may even be standing in the way of economic deals highly desirable from a political point of view. This, together with the fact that the Soviet bloc requires few oil imports, handicaps them in making trade arrangements with Iraq.

One of the unknown factors relevant to the assessment of export surpluses of the Soviet bloc is the effect of changes in the direction and extent of military spending. It is hard to speculate on this, and harder still to estimate how far the internal output and utilization plans within the bloc have already been adjusted to such changes. However, because of the relevance of this to the production and consumption of a number of key commodities entering world trade, the point must be made.

Thus the potential political and economic advantages of trade expansion conflict with long-ingrown habits of Soviet economic and planning policy. We can anticipate strong arguments at the political level, between those who wish to take advantage of external economic and political opportunities and those who give their primary attention to internal growth. So far, despite all that has happened recently, internal developments have tended to come first. There should be a steady intensification of bloc trading activities, but not the continuation of the remarkable rate of increase of the last few years, since this was from artificially depressed levels.

The USSR will no doubt come to play a larger role as an exporter of machinery, and the industrialized satellites will take opportunities to expand into Latin America. But, against the background of the vast needs of the underdeveloped world as a whole, this will hardly transform the existing situation. The West will continue to be the principal trading partner of these countries--except in such probably temporary instances as Egypt and Iceland, where the Soviet bloc was able to step into a trade vacuum created by circumstances. But, naturally, if one of these countries were to fall under a purely pro-Soviet regime, one would expect the bloc to make big efforts to keep such a new regime on an even keel economically.

Some observers would regard this analysis as too "conservative," or insufficiently alarmist. If the Soviet bloc is growing rapidly in economic might, as it certainly is, then quite a small increment of additional production would be sufficient to permit a substantial growth of exports, while internal demand must also expand. Thus the USSR at present exports only 3 percent of its national income in the Soviet definition, 27/ less than this in the Western definition. Even if this small percentage remained constant, the share of the USSR in world trade must grow. Only a very small proportion of the exports of the USSR, and of other members of the bloc, are at present directed at underdeveloped countries. Surely, it may be argued, great opportunities exist.

No doubt they do. No doubt the relative share of the bloc in world trade will grow. However, export capability is not a question only of increased production, but must be related to internal demand. An increase of, say, 100 percent in the productive capacity of the Soviet chemical industry will not affect export availabilities at all, if internal utilization is planned to increase to the same extent. Indeed, this particular development may actually reduce Soviet participation in world trade by reducing demand for certain imported materials.

In general, therefore, one could anticipate more trade of kinds which give the bloc some economic advantage, but with relatively little sacrifice of effort and resources. Of course, not all trade is necessarily advantageous (thus it is probable that more rice and cotton were purchased from Burma and Egypt respectively than was strictly necessary) and, as stated before, not all transactions described as "aid" involve any appreciable sacrifice.

It may well be that, in the last analysis, the West's principal danger lies more in the indirect effects of Soviet growth on the internal politics of underdeveloped countries--plus much-publicized, selective and relatively inexpensive deals--than in our being subjected to an all-out economic offensive. However, all this depends, once again, on political decision. No one can doubt that the bloc's potential for economic warfare is constantly increasing, and the danger exists that it can be one day brought fully into play; indeed, one of the political objects of the policy of maximizing internal growth may be to make possible just such an offensive in the long term.

CONCLUSION

The following general conclusions seem to emerge from the analysis-- although in the nature of things they must be seen as just tentative approximations about probable tendencies in an uncertain world.

It seems clear that the Soviet bloc economy will continue to grow considerably faster than that of the West. However, not only will the pace of growth, except in China, be slower than hitherto, but it will also require great efforts and cause very considerable strains to maintain even this reduced growth rate in the next decade. The difficulties will in part be physical, connected with the development of more remote sources of materials, with a tendency towards diminishing returns in many sectors of the economy. They will also be social-political. While the determination of the leadership to run the race with the West will presumably remain constant, the necessity of providing incentives, of ensuring the indispensable minimum of collaboration from the citizenry, is leading to a diversion of resources into nongrowth-inducing sectors. This diversion must appear to the leadership as an essential or inevitable part of the program of growth, but must tend to contribute to the slow-down in the rate of advance. It becomes--particularly in the satellites, but also in the USSR itself--part of the price of political stability and the stimulation of effort.

The Soviet bloc regimes are also finding it necessary to devise new methods, to find a new balance between central planning and local initiative, between party domination and the autonomy of management. This balance must be found if scarce resources, especially labor, are to be used with maximum effect, and it remains to be seen whether the various obstacles in the way can be satisfactorily overcome. There is an intimate connection between this problem and the shift towards incentives and away from crude coercion as the basis of planning. China, however, seems likely to proceed on its own path with a degree of social coercion remarkable even by Stalinist standards.

All this increases the pressure on available investment resources, thereby limiting the central planners' freedom of action. In such a situation, their natural tendency to give priority to internal needs, to plan for self-sufficiency, may be reinforced. Likely victims of investment cuts will be those projects which could provide an export surplus for disposal on uncertain world markets. There will surely be a tendency to invest in the less risky projects which will supply the internal needs of the bloc, which can be made the basis of long-term agreements. Therefore, intrabloc exchanges, based on a planned specialization, should continue to dominate Soviet trade, while bloc exchanges with the outside world may be severely limited by the relative shortage of exportable surpluses.

Notably the rapidly increasing output of capital goods will be very largely earmarked for the bloc's own capital projects. This relative scarcity of capital goods for export, rather than lack of specifically financial capability, must be expected to be a major limiting factor in Soviet bloc aid. The expansion of the total size of the economy need not give rise to a proportionate increase in export capabilities, if this expansion is closely geared to internal needs. Nor does the freeing of resources by

62

reduced military requirements change the situation in the longer run. There doubtless arises an immediate surplus of certain items for which there was an appreciable military demand; but in view of the many claimants on scarce investment resources, the effect may be to hold back expansion of the given item until civilian demand has taken up the slack.

The bloc countries appear to be planning mutual cooperation, with coordination of long-term investment projects; the industrially more developed will be committed to help underdeveloped bloc countries in the first instance. Of these, much the most important is, of course, China. While bloc cooperation will doubtless encounter many obstacles, and lead to frictions and disputes, interdependence will surely grow, and the availabilities for the outside world, including nonbloc underdeveloped countries, may be correspondingly restricted.

These considerations by no means exclude an aid drive being directed at any one country, where big political advantages may be had at low cost. Nor is there much doubt that a considerable expansion of trade with nonbloc countries from the present levels is possible, indeed probable. Such trade is at an unnaturally low level, and rising import requirements will compel the setting aside of resources for export so as to pay for them. Imports of a number of useful but nonessential goods can be expanded or contracted as the political situation requires, providing valuable (though still somewhat limited) elbowroom for politico-economic deals which cost little or nothing, but enable the bloc to claim the role of benefactor vis-à-vis certain underdeveloped countries. The latter, searching for safe markets, are bound to be tempted by Soviet offers, especially long-term contracts. The limiting factor, to repeat, seems to be export surpluses or, in the longer run, investment within the bloc in export capacity.

Thus the problem of Soviet aid and trade drives is essentially a matter not of abstract "capabilities," which obviously exist and will increase with the growth of the economy as a whole; it is a question of decisions about priorities, in a situation where competing claims on scarce resources will be strongly pressed. The effect of the cold war on the choices between priorities is by no means clear. On the one hand it is of positive value to the Communist leadership, since it maintains cohesion, and provides both a stimulus to and an explanation for sacrifice and effort. Political trade and aid deals are encouraged, in a search for quick results on the cold-war front. Against this, the cold war reinforces autarkic tendencies and thereby restricts trade, and by tying up more resources in armaments increases the demand for resources within the bloc.

The role of China, both as a power in her own right and as a source of attraction to other Asian countries, seems likely to develop extremely rapidly. The combination of rapid growth with an original, but ruthless, approach to production and organizational problems, will cause many minds in underdeveloped countries to examine the Chinese model (although some may well be repelled by what they see). China's increasing might and rapidly expanding population may conceivably bring her into ultimate conflict with the Soviet Union, and in fact there may already be a kind of "competitive coexistence" or "race to communism" between the two giant Communist powers; but speculation on such matters lies outside the scope of this paper.

Although we must expect to see more examples of the selective use of trade and aid in some "sensitive" areas, such as the Middle East, there is little likelihood, on present evidence, of a devastating all-out trade-and-aid drive by the Soviet bloc. The developed satellites must be expected to try to sell more in overseas markets, but much of this is likely to consist of straight commercial deals, designed to earn foreign currency, and it is surely true that the effect of a purchase of Czech or East German goods is much smaller in influencing Asian or African minds in a pro-communist direction, than the effect of a deal with Russia or China.

The really serious danger lies in the influence of Soviet-bloc might on the minds of men, and trade as such is not necessarily the only or even the most important way to achieve this. Khrushchev and his colleagues believe in a vulgarized Marxism, and tend to the view that their methods are bound to seem irresistibly attractive once they achieve an economic stature comparable with the United States and its allies. They also believe that the West is bound to founder under its own inner contradictions. They are optimistic that the many difficult internal problems can be overcome; they give priority attention to internal questions. Their economic strategy-- and indeed their political strategy too--is based on the long haul, not the all-out offensive in the short run.

Fortunately for the West, it is by no means clear whether the Soviet bloc countries will be able to overcome the many practical problems facing them, while maintaining intact the political-ideological system which keeps them running in the economic race and keeps the bloc together. The current "struggle against revisionism" is one aspect of the dilemma: How can one ensure the necessary mental initiative at official and working levels while simultaneously repressing the expression of unorthodox thought? How can arbitrary party rule be combined with economic rationality?

Thus it would be unreasonable to view the situation in a spirit of defeatism, as if the Soviet world had either limitless resources or a magic formula for success, or to fail to observe the many difficult social and economic problems which the leadership must face. On the other hand, too much stress on difficulties would encourage an equally unreasonable spirit of complacency. In terms of production, we shall indeed soon have the Soviet bloc breathing down our necks; they are catching up fast, if not as fast as they claim. Despite some softening of attitudes towards citizens' needs, the Soviet countries are able to devote a high proportion of their national income to investment, and, although the planning system suffers from imperfections, an uninterrupted and rapid growth rate should be achieved--subject to the avoidance of major political blunders. Problems are not insoluble, and economic difficulties are by no means confined to the Soviet bloc.

Soviet industrial output seems likely to double in roughly 10 years, national income in 14 or so. This would be undeniably very impressive, by any standard. The relative increase in the economic power of the Soviet world must add to its attractiveness as an example, to its military potential, and to the capability of using economic weapons to achieve political ends. It is true that relatively few resources are being devoted to the waging of economic warfare, but we already know that aid programs of moderate size can have a quite disproportionate political effect. No country is likely to be won for the Soviet bloc by economic means alone. Yet there can be little doubt that the might of the bloc, the knowledge that it can supply the sinews of industrialization, could decisively influence internal developments in uncommitted countries, without anything which could be called Soviet intervention.

The problem--and it is a serious problem--is to strike a proper balance in conclusion. The Soviet economic challenge is real and formidable, and this must be clearly stated. However, in this world of overdramatized propaganda, this leads too easily into a state of mind in which every Soviet economic decision becomes part of a fiendishly clever design for world conquest. Those who work and organize the Soviet economic system are predominantly motivated by a desire to build up the greatness and prosperity of their countries, as well as by material gain. Most of their acts are explicable in these terms. It is true that the top Communist leadership has world-wide ambitions and uses the feelings of patriotism and the material ambitions of its subjects to further its own ends. But how long will it be before the leadership is itself "infected" by the ideas already predominant among its own bureaucracy and technicians? Higher living standards in Soviet countries could well stimulate such a tendency. Cassius, it will be recalled, had a lean and hungry look. 1/

Finally, so much depends on what the West does. Just as, in the struggle for Africa, the events, say, in Nyasaland are more effective than many years of Communist propaganda, so American restrictions on commodity imports or a recession which causes a sharp drop in raw material prices, may do more to provide economic and political opportunities to the Communists than any trade maneuver yet devised by Mikoyan. Indeed, it is just these things which Soviet ideologists call the inevitable contradictions of capitalism in its imperialist stage of decay. If the West in its behavior conforms to their theories, we will have only ourselves to blame for the consequences.

APPENDIX TABLES

Table 1

OUTPUT OF MAJOR COMMODITIES, INTERNATIONAL COMPARISON, 1913–57

	1913	1937	1950	1956	1957
Coal (incl. lignite)					
(million tons)					
USSR	29	128	261	429	463
United States	517	451	508	480	470
Great Britain	292	244	220	226	227
West Germany	n.a.	203	187	230	230
China	–	62	39	105	n.a.
Oil (excl. gas) (million tons)					
USSR	9	28	38	84	98
United States	34	173	267	353	354
Venezuela	–	27	80	129	148
Electric energy (billion kwh)a/					
USSR	2	36	91	192	210
United States	22	146	389	684	716
Great Britain	4	32	63	96	100
Steel (million tons)					
USSR	4.2	17.7	27.3	48.6	51.0
United States	31.8	51.4	87.8	104.3	102.3
West Germany	n.a.	15.6	12.1	23.6	24.5
Great Britain	7.8	13.2	16.6	21.0	22.0
Automobiles and trucks (thous.)					
USSR	–	200	363	465	495
United States	485	4809	8003	6906	7220
Great Britain	34	504	784	1004	1149
West Germany	n.a.	261	305	1073	1212
Tractors (thous.)					
USSR	1b/	51	109	184	204
United States	171b/	238	509	374c/	n.a.
Great Britain	–	18	120	132	n.a.
France	–	2	14	78	n.a.

Table 1, Continued

	1913	1937	1950	1956	1957
Caustic soda (thous. tons)					
USSR	55	164	325	631	n.a.
United States	n.a.	879	2278	3822	n.a.
West Germany	n.a.	n.a.	355	594	n.a.
Cement (million tons)					
USSR	1.5	5.5	10.2	24.9	28.8
United States	15.9	19.8	38.0	55.1	52.6
West Germany	n.a.	8.5	10.9	20.5	19.2
Japan	0.7	6.1	4.5	12.9	15.1
Cotton fabrics (billion meters)					
USSR	2.6	3.4	3.9	5.5	5.6
United States	5.7	7.9	9.2	9.4	8.7
Great Britain	7.4	3.3	1.9	1.5	1.5
India	n.a.	3.7	3.4	4.9	4.9
Japan	0.4	4.0	1.3	2.9	3.2

a/ Soviet figures include current used at stations, and should be reduced by
   roughly 6-7 percent to achieve comparability.
b/ 1928
c/ 1955

Table 2

OUTPUT OF SELECTED COMMODITIES, USSR, 1937-58, and PLANNED TARGETS, 1965

	1937	1950	1955	1957	1958	1965 targets
Pig iron (mill. tons)	15	19	33	37	39.6	67.5
Steel (mill. tons)	18	27	45	51	54.9	88.5
Rolling mill products (mill. tons)	13	21	35	40	42.9	67.5
Iron ore (mill. tons)	28	40	72	84	88.8	155
Coal and lignite (mill. tons)	128	261	391	463	496	606
Oil (mill. tons)	29	38	71	98	113	235
Natural gas (bill. cub. met.)	2.3	6.2	10.4	20.2	29.8	150
Electricity (bill. kwh)	36	91	170	210	233	510
Mineral fertilizer (gross) (mill. tons)	3.2	5.5	9.6	11.7	12.4	(36)
Sulphuric acid (thous. tons)	1,369	2,125	3,798	4,569	4,800	n.a.
Machine tools (thous. units)	49	71	117	131	138	195
Metallurgical equipment (thous. tons)	18	111	172	164	173	-
Forging and stamping machines (thous.units)	3	9	19	228	24.6	36
Turbines (mill. kw)	-	2.7	5.5	5.4	6.6	19.5
Steam locomotives (units)	1,172	985	654	n.a.	n.a.	0
Diesel locomotives (units)	4	125	134	400	712⎫	
Electric locomotives (units)	32	102	194	270	344⎭	2,625
Goods wagons (rail) (thous.)	30	51	34	38	40.3	-
Automobiles and trucks (thous.)	200	363	445	495	511	800
Tractors (thous.)	51	109	163	204	220	-
Grain combines (thous.)	44	46	48	131	65	-
Timber haulage (mill. cub. met.)	114	161	212	235	235a/	277.5
Cement (mill. tons)	6	10	23	29	33.3	78
Cotton fabrics (mill. met.)	3,448	3,889	5,905	5,595	5,800	7,850
Wool fabrics (mill. met.)	108	155	252	282	303	500
Silk and rayon fabrics (mill. met.)	59	130	526	805	845	1,485
Linen fabrics (mill. met.)	286	282	306	425	481	635
Leather footwear (mill. pairs)	183	203	275	315	356	515
Clocks and watches (millions)	4	8	20	24	25	35.5
Sewing machines, domestic (thous.)	510	502	1,611	2,267	2,700	4,550
Bicycles (thous.)	541	649	2,884	3,318	3,700	-
Paper (thous. tons)	832	1,193	1,862	2,125	2,200	3,500
Sugar (thous. tons)	2,421	2,523	3,419	4,491	5,400	9,625

a/ Excluding collective farms.

Sources: Statistical Yearbooks to 1956, Vestnik Statistiki, No. 5/1958 for 1957; plan and policy declarations for 1965. Planovoe Khozaistvo, No. 5/ 1959; 1958: Pravda, January 16, 1959.

Note: 1965 figures are generally midpoints of ranges.

Table 3a

AGRICULTURAL PRODUCTION, USSR, 1928-58 AND PLANNED 1965
(Million metric tons)

	1928	1950	1953	1956	1957	1958	1965 (targets)a/
Grain	73.1	(84)	88	(115)	(100)	(125)	172
Potatoes	42.2	88.6e/	72.6	96.0d/	87.8e/	86.1	147
Sunflower seed	2.2	2.0	2.6	4.1	n.a.	4.5	n.a.
Cotton	0.7	3.6	3.9	4.5	4.2f/	4.4	5.9
Sugar-beet	10.1	20.8e/	23.2	32.5	39.7	54.1	80
Milkb/	30.1	35.3	36.7	49.2	54.7	57.8	102.5
Meatc/	(5.0)d/	4.9	5.8	6.5	7.3	7.9	16
Wool	0.18	0.18	0.23	0.26	0.29	0.32	0.55

a/ Midpoints of range.
b/ Figures for 1950 and after are exaggerated and include noncow milk.
c/ Figures for 1950 and after are exaggerated and include offal, lard, poultry, rabbits.
d/ The official figure for that year (3.6) has been arbitrarily increased to give it the same product coverage as for the later years.

Sources: 1928 official data, taken from Dr. N. Jasny's Socialised Agriculture of the USSR (pre-1939 territory). Except where stated below, other data were given in Pravda, January 16, 1959 or were derived by official output indices.
e/ Kommunist No. 13/1958.
f/ Pravda, February 18, 1958.

Note on the grain figures: The official figures given for 1958 (139 million tons) and implied for 1956 (126 million tons) are too high and have been replaced by estimates. Undefined amendments to the previously published index of grain production make the figures for 1956 and 1957 doubtful. The 1953 figure was given by Khrushchev, Pravda, December 16, 1958.

Table 3b

USSR LIVESTOCK POPULATION (present territory) 1916-1958
(million heads)

	Jan. 1916	Jan. 1928	Jan. 1951	Jan. 1953	Jan. 1956	Jan. 1958	Dec. 1958
Cattle	58.4	66.8	57.1	56.6	58.8	66.7	70.8
Cows	28.8	33.2	24.3	24.3	27.7	31.4	33.3
Pigs	23.0	27.7	24.4	28.5	34.0	44.3	48.5
Sheep	89.7	a/	82.6	94.2	103.3	120.1	129.6

a/ Cannot separate sheep from goats.

Source: Figures for January 1928, 1951 and 1953: Narodnoe Khozyaistvo SSSR, 1956. Figures for January 1956, 1958: Vestnik Statistiki, No. 4/ 1958. Figures for December 1958: Pravda, January 16, 1959. Figures for January 1916: Chislennost Skota v SSSR.

Table 4

USSR: STATE BUYING PRICES FOR FARM PRODUCE, 1952-58
(Collective farms and private individuals)
(Rubles per quintal-100 kilograms)

	1952		1953/55		1956			1957	1958
	A	B	A	B	A	B	C	C	Single Price
Grain (average)	9	16	20 a/	80 a/	20	80	53	53	74
Potatoes	4	30	10	30	33	53	n.a.	n.a.	40
Beef (live weight)	30	300	150	410	150	410	} 360	302	619
Pork (live weight)	60	540	320	700	320	700		n.a.	786
Milk	27	80	55	120	55	120	97	102	115
Cotton	--	--	--	--	--	--	372	366	340

A Compulsory delivery price.

B Over-quota delivery price (very little bought at this price before 1953).

C Weighted average of prices paid to collective farms.

a/ These prices were paid from 1955.

Source: The September 1953 decrees. Pravda, February 2, 1956, January 25, 1958, July 1, 1958; Tresorukova, Vestnik Statistiki, No. 4/ 1959, p. 11.

Note: All the figures are averages, with marked regional and seasonal variations. The grain prices for 1952 are very approximate. The prices of 1958 have to cover also the costs of machinery transferred from the MTS.

Table 5a

PATTERN OF SOVIET FOREIGN TRADE, 1955-57
by Country
(Millions "valuta" rubles, approximately
convertible at 4R = $1)

	Imports				Exports		
	1955	1956	1957		1955	1956	1957
Total	12,242	14,453	15,751		13,874	14,446	17,526
(a) Intrabloc, Total	9,604	10,744	11,075		10,827	10,642	12,925
Albania	22	33	56		61	73	131
Bulgaria	486	579	792		510	434	690
China	2,574	3,057	2,953		2,993	2,932	2,176
Czechoslovakia	1,546	1,586	1,542		1,424	1,495	2,205
East Germany	2,026	2,505	3,057		1,915	2,285	3,448
Hungary	586	483	427		461	507	999
Mongolia	215	217	201		487	414	271
North Korea	163	205	250		177	215	240
North Vietnam	0	5	13		1	10	39
Poland	1,147	1,133	1,024		1,727	1,429	1,723
Rumania	839	941	760		1,071	848	1,003
(b) Nonbloc, Total	2,638	3,709	4,676		3,047	3,804	4,601
Austria	142	258	272		55	44	72
Belgium	61	128	123		97	117	113
Denmark	40	26	46		31	33	52
Finland	511	585	661		425	459	602
France	144	202	190		239	279	268
Germany (West)	95	272	247		117	167	286
Greece	9	25	38		17	29	49
Netherlands	134	40	82		131	167	131
Iceland	40	50	55		41	40	46
Italy	65	104	182		70	136	117
Norway	60	86	72		70	78	84
Sweden	68	104	101		114	139	126
Switzerland	16	8	15		34	46	40
United Kingdom	284	298	448		677	593	756
Yugoslavia	70	199	227		66	276	292
Afghanistan	44	61	83		54	73	73
Burma	67	49	36		1	17	26
India	18	73	168		29	162	339
Indonesia	15	52	79		0	1	22
Iran	76	61	74		90	77	127
Japan	7	3	35		9	12	34
Lebanon	4	7	6		5	7	9
Malaya	87	336	195		0	1	2
Pakistan	0	3	21		1	1	7
Syria	--	6	22		1	6	18
Turkey	21	26	22		30	24	36

Table 5a, Continued

	Imports				Exports		
	1955	1956	1957		1955	1956	1957
Algeria	--	--	--		--	7	15
Egypt	62	201	444		44	154	329
Ethiopia	0	1	11		0	0	1
Ghana	46	33	76		0	0	0
Morocco	--	4	21		--	6	3
Sudan	--	--	12		--	2	3
Union of South Africa	38	51	107		0	2	1
Canada	11	98	36		8	9	17
United States	2	19	41		95	109	64
Argentina	113	52	83		96	77	19
Cuba	143	59	188		--	--	--
Uruguay	40	49	73		1	11	1
New Zealand	16	34	32		0	0	0

Source: Vneshnaya Torgovlya SSSR

Table 5b

PRINCIPAL COMMODITIES ENTERING SOVIET FOREIGN TRADE, 1938-57
(Quantities in thousand metric tons,
except where otherwise stated)

Exports	1938	1950	1955	1957
Coal	52	1,024	2,875	6,997
Anthracite	371	97	1,437	1,775
Coke	--	658	1,617	2,196
Oil (crude) }	1,400	1,100	2,916	5,923
Oil products }			5,070	7,758
Iron ore	7	3,227	8,818	10,773
Manganese ore	446	227	851	806
Pig iron	6	398	1,149	1,278
Rolled steel	53	584	1,511	1,923
Pipes	3	62	186	207
Sawmill products (thous. cub. met.)	3,209	1,042	2,338	3,457
Pulp (thous. cub. met.)	1,127	197	547	591
Pit-props (thous. cub. met.)	1,259	378	839	817
Raw cotton	20	216	337	319
Grain	2,000	2,900	3,683	7,414
Machinery and equipment (mill. rubles)	51	850	2,396	2,609
Imports				
Machinery and equipment (mill. rubles)	376	1,252	3,701	3,762
of which:				
Machine tools (mill. rubles)	153	61	97	129
Railroad equipment (mill. rubles)	0.2	296	460	578
Ships and parts (mill. rubles)	28	115	1,055	958
Coal	--	8,800	8,664	3,423
Oil (crude) }	--	2,600	575	1,331
Oil products }			3,816	2,937
Rolled steel	88	185	86	723
Raw cotton	16	45	20	109
Wool	23	35	47	57
Grain	129	207	306	153
Rice	40	40	487	371
Oilseeds	3	530	760	716
Meat and products	3	47	239	117
Fresh fruit and berries	34	3	133	218
Tea	17	6	10	21
Cocoa beans	15	12	14	44
Sugar	--	358	933	645
Clothing (mill. rubles)	--	5	90	587

Sources: 1938 and 1950: Vneshnaya Torgovlya No. 11/1957 and No. 4/1958. 1955 and 1957: Vneshnaya Torgovlya SSSR (the official trade returns).

Note: Sums in rubles, where given, are expressed in the then current world prices, converted at the then current official exchange rate (5 R = $1.00 in 1938, 4 R = $1.00 in other years).

The total volume of trade turnover in 1957 was officially stated to be 6.2 times that of 1938, giving a rough price index of 250.

NOTES

Introduction

1. See Joseph S. Berliner, Soviet Economic Aid, Praeger, 1958, pp. 140 ff.

Chapter One

1. It is, however, arguable that terror was inescapably connected with the process of industrialization, because it alone enables an "industrializing" government to get control of the necessary rural surpluses. Indeed, this is the economic explanation of Stalinism.
2. Planovoe Khozaistvo, No. 11/1957, p. 82.

Chapter Two

1. For instance, D. Shimkin, Minerals, a Key to Soviet Power, Harvard University Press, Cambridge, Mass., 1953; Professor Chauncey Harris's contribution in A. Bergson, ed., Soviet Economic Growth, Evanston, Ill., Row, Peterson, 1953; and M. Gardner Clark, Economics of Soviet Steel, Harvard University Press, Cambridge, Mass., 1956.
2. Kostennikov, Planovoe Khozaistvo, op. cit., No. 1/1959, p. 75.
3. According to Planovoe Khozaistvo, op. cit., No. 9/1958, p. 7, there are to be 26,000 kilometers of gas pipelines built in the period 1959-65. A major oil pipeline from the Ural-Bashkir oilfield is to extend to Irkutsk.
4. Shimkin, op. cit., p. 304.
5. The actual tonnage claimed by Peking is scarcely credible, but it was certainly a very good harvest. See A. Doak Barnett, Communist Economic Strategy: The Rise of Mainland China, National Planning Association, Washington, D. C., 1959, especially Chapters Five and Seven.
6. See Appendix Table 4.
7. See his speech reported in Pravda, Moscow, June 21, 1958. There is plenty of evidence that grain yields of only half a ton per hectare are quite usual in these areas at present. Podsol soils, affected by centuries of coniferous trees, have a high acidity and low natural fertility.
8. See prices in Appendix Table 4.
9. See Norman M. Kaplan, "Capital Formation and Allocation," in Abram Bergson, ed., Soviet Economic Growth, op. cit.
10. See Berliner's excellent book, Factory and Manager in the USSR, Harvard University Press, Cambridge, Mass., 1957, for discussion of safety margins.
11. Ovechkin, Trudnaya Vesna, Novyi Mir, No. 9, 1956, p. 126. For a more recent attack on party orders which disrupt rotation plans, see Granin in Oktyabr No. 9/1958.
12. Khachaturov, in Kommunist, No. 8/1957, p. 40.
13. According to Pravda, Moscow, August 2, 1957, and November 14, 1958, house construction is to be as follows, in millions of square meters of total space:

	1957	1960	Annual Averages 1952-58	1959-65 Plan
By state institutions	34	60)	40	93
By individuals and coops	13	41)		

(These figures exclude peasants' houses built by peasants.)

Notes to Chapter Two, Continued

14. See Appendix Table 2.
15. See Kuzmin, Vestnik Akademii Nauk, No. 6/1958.
16. Although not all Soviet economists think so. Thus Strumilin criticized the pattern of the plan in Literaturnaya Gazeta, December 2, 1958. However, we should not too readily accept every critical utterance by even so eminent a Soviet economist. In fact, unanimity is more suspect (and much less healthy) than open disagreement.
17. According to Starovski, Kommunist, No. 7/1959, p. 78, in the period 1939-59 the increase in the urban population from 60.4 to 99.8 million was composed as follows: 24-25 million persons moved from village to town, 7 million were residents of former villages which became towns, and there was a net natural increase of 8 million in towns.
18. Partiinaya Zhizn, No. 13/1957, p. 27.
19. Well-qualified managers, engineers, mechanics, party officials were sent to the Machine Tractor Stations in and after 1953.
20. Since 1956, there has been a two-hour cut in Saturday work, with some further reductions in selected industries.
21. It is likely that the intolerable waste of skills in the labor camps contributed, in the context of labor shortage, to the decision to release most of the inmates.
22. See Barnett, op. cit.
23. Details may be found in Korol's Soviet Education for Science and Technology, Cambridge, Mass., Technology Press, M.I.T., 1957. However, standards may be lowered as part of the present reform.

Chapter Three

1. For an invaluable discussion of all these matters, readers are referred to the symposium on "Economic Calculation and Organization in Eastern Europe," (University of California, Berkeley), slated to be published during 1959.
2. For example, freight charges for Moscow basin coal were halved in 1950 "to encourage its use," Maisenberg, Tseno-obrazovanie v narodom Khozaistve SSSR, 1953, p. 247.
3. The reform has tended to strengthen the party organs in the localities, but these are just as likely as the regional authorities to give priority to their region's needs. Some particularly striking examples have been given in the party press; See an unsigned article in Kommunist, No. 12/1958, p. 37.
4. China now is making some very interesting experiments with regionalism.
5. The important trends towards reform in economic theory and practice in Poland, Czechoslovakia, and in some other bloc countries deserve much fuller treatment than they can possibly receive here.
6. This thought is developed at some length in the present author's article, "The Politics of Economic Rationality," in Social Research, Vol. 25, No. 2, summer 1958, p. 127.
7. The best Soviet summary of the present state of the Soviet debate on value and prices is by Kulikov in Voprosy Ekonomiki No. 8/1958. For a full report of one such debate, see Zakon Stoimasti i evo rol' pri sotsializme, Gosplan editors, Moscow, 1959.
8. The Political Economy of Socialism, Polish Institute of International Affairs, Warsaw, 1958, mimeographed, p. 16.

9. See articles by Nemchinov and by Liberman in Kommunist No. 1/1959.
10. See, for instance, Nemchinov's article in Voprosy Ekonomiki, No. 4/1959.
11. The Russians are showing great interest in linear programming and the use of electronic computors, as possible means of "saving" central planning.
12. See Appendix Table 4.
13. Except that large specialized machines, and repair workshops, are supposed to be operated by state-run Repair Technical Stations (RTS). These are proving unpopular, and many farms have their own workshops and do not use those of the RTS.
14. Rovinskii, Novyi Mir, No. 8/1957, p. 208.
15. Not to mention serious novels, such as Dudintsev's Not by Bread Alone, New York, E.P. Dutton & Co., Inc., 1957.
16. One example among a great many: The inventor of an efficient small boiler found that no factory would touch it, because the boiler output plan was expressed in terms of heating surface, so that the adoption of the invention would make it more difficult to fulfill the plan. Pravda, September 5, 1958.

Chapter Four

1. Yoffe, Strany Sotsialisma i Kapitalisma v Tsifrakh, Moscow, 1957, p. 48.
2. 53-55 percent, according to Mirovaya Ekonomika i Mezhdunarodnye Otnoshenia, No. 2/1959, p. 11.
3. Na Putyakh Postroenia Kommunizma, Moscow, 1959, p. 38.
4. Economic Journal, March 1957, pp. 83-104.
5. Khachaturov, Kommunist No. 8/1957, p. 38. This seems somewhat too high, but the truth cannot be far below this; according to Shimkin it is 35 percent, excluding metal-working.
6. This does not do sufficient justice to the subtlety of his methods, which are set out in detail in his paper, op. cit.
7. Strumilin, op. cit., and the League of Nations' Industrialization and Foreign Trade, Geneva 1945, p. 13, both reached this conclusion, on what looks like sound evidence.
8. For a Soviet analysis of the causes of the slowdown in the period 1937-40, see Istoriya SSSR, No. 1/1959.
9. One further factor which may make the slowdown seem greater than it really is arises from the fact that 1951-55 growth statistics were expressed in the prices of 1952, which gave a higher weight to the rapidly growing machinery sector than did the prices of 1955, in which all later indexes are calculated.
10. For instance, among hundreds of similar claims: "In 10 days 4,350 iron and steel, machinery, chemical fertilizer, cement, and other factories were built" in one rural district in Honan (italics added), Hung Chi, 1 Sept. 1958, quoted from translation by the U.S. Consulate-General, Hongkong.
11. In the Rockefeller Brothers Fund report, Foreign Economic Policy for the Twentieth Century, New York, 1958, the strange forecast is made that China's GNP will rise by 2 percent per annum. Surely this is one forecast which its authors will wish to forget! For a discussion of Chinese growth rates, see Barnett, op. cit., Chapter Two.
12. These arguments have been made in detail in the works of Simon Kuznets.

13. However, some cut in cotton prices has recently occurred. See Appendix Table 4.

14. They are generally responsible for local retailing arrangements, small-scale workshops, cafes, entertainments, etc., as well as drainage, house repairs, water supply, paving, lighting, urban transportation; and these things can make a great difference in peoples' lives.

15. The subject of this and subsequent paragraphs is discussed extensively in Jan Wszelaki, Communist Economic Strategy: The Role of East-Central Europe, National Planning Association, Washington, D. C., 1959.

16. The Political Economy of Socialism, Polish Institute of International Affairs, mimeographed, 1958, p. 35.

17. The Council for Mutual Economic Assistance, the coordinating body for the European Soviet-bloc economies. China is represented by an observer.

18. Mirovaya Ekonomika i Mezhdunarodnye Otnoshenia, No. 4/1959, pp. 23-31.

19. For a discussion of Sino-Soviet trade, see Barnett, op. cit., Chapter Eight.

20. See Appendix Table 5a.

21. This whole problem is analyzed in some detail by J. Marczewski in his interesting first chapter of Planification et croissance économique des démocraties populaires, Paris, 1955.

22. Economic Change, London, 1954, p. 246.

23. In 1930-33, Soviet farm output fell sharply. Chinese production seems to be rising fairly rapidly.

24. Aid was given to Yugoslavia on terms which suggested that she was being treated as a quasi-member of the Soviet bloc. This may explain why it was suspended when political quarrels reopened. It may be more logical, therefore, to exclude Yugoslavia.

25. These points, and others, are argued convincingly and in detail by Berliner, Soviet Economic Aid, op. cit.

26. See, in this connection, Jan Wszelaki, Communist Economic Strategy: the Role of East-Central Europe, National Planning Association, Washington, 1959.

27. Calculated by Bogomolov and analyzed by Nove and Zauberman in Soviet Studies, October 1958. The relatively much greater importance of foreign trade to other members of the bloc is illustrated by the following figures, in foreign-trade rubles (4R = $1.00):

Trade turnover per capita, 1957

USSR	166
Rumania	180
Poland	312
Hungary	472
East Germany	787
Czechoslovakia	817
China	19

Source: Mirovaya Ekonomika i Mezhdunarodnye Otnoshenia, No. 4/1959, p. 31.

Note to Conclusion

1. This argument led Professor Gerschenkron, in his contribution to the symposium on Bergson, ed. Soviet Economic Growth, op. cit., to put forward the view that the Soviet leaders may avoid improving the standard of living, in order to maintain dynamism. However, steps to improve living standards are in fact unavoidable.

81

82